COMPETITIVE
CLAY TARGET SHOOTING

COMPETITIVE
CLAY TARGET SHOOTING

Paul Bentley

A & C Black · London

First published 1991 by
A & C Black (Publishers) Ltd
35 Bedford Row, London WC1R 4JH

© 1991 Paul Bentley

ISBN 0 7136 3406 5

A CIP catalogue record for this book
is available from the British Library.

Printed and bound in Great Britain
by Butler & Tanner Ltd, Frome and
London.

Contents

*'The spoils of war!' Mickey Rouse with the British Open Sporting
championship cup*

Introduction

In recent years the sport of clay target shooting has experienced an unprecedented worldwide growth that could hardly have been predicted ten years ago. From a game that began life as a humble substitute for the 'real thing', clay shooting has developed an identity of its own, having long ago shed its rather down market 'cloth cap' image. People from all walks of life now enjoy clay shooting for its own sake, and it is likely that a fair percentage of them never shoot at a live target, nor have any wish to do so.

Like any sport, clay shooting may be enjoyed at many levels. At one end of the scale can be a person who enjoys shooting just 25 targets every other weekend. At the opposite end will be a dedicated sportsman who spends much of his spare time (and a fair portion of his disposable income) attempting to attain the highest performance level of which he is capable. He will often fire upwards of 15,000 cartridges each year.

The ambition of a shooter of this standard will be to win major national championships, ultimately to make his national team and represent his country at European, world and Olympic level. The highest achievement, of course, is to win one of these prestigious championships, or a place medal.

Competitive clay shooting is divided into several so-called disciplines, each of which has several sub-disciplines. The three main disciplines are Sporting, Skeet and Trap.

Sporting is the most natural of the three in that the targets are thrown to simulate the multivariable flight possibilities of real birds. Thus almost anything that is airborne or bowling along the ground, provided it is within shotgun range, can fairly be called a Sporting target. Most Sporting stands involve the shooting of doubles, making the possible target combinations very testing shooting.

At club level, the setting up of a simple but interesting Sporting layout requires no more than a few clay traps, a suitable field, and some imagination. It is this fact, coupled with the almost endless variety of targets that can be encountered at the various shoots, that makes Sporting the most popular discipline of all. There are two main Sporting disciplines: the domestic version, English Sporting, which is the most common and popular; and the international variant, FITASC Sporting, which is expensive to shoot and very testing.

Skeet is the most recently established of the three disciplines. A precise description of a Skeet range will be found in the chapter on Skeet. Hitting all 25 targets in a round of Skeet is little cause for celebration to a top shooter, although he will be far more enthusiastic if he manages to break all 100 in a four-round competition! For the newcomer to the sport, his first '25 straight' will be an event he remembers for the rest of his shooting career, every bit as vividly as the first time, should he ever do so, that he breaks his first '100 straight'.

Trap shooting is the oldest of the clay target games, having had its origins in live pigeon shooting. This rather barbarous practice involved the use of live pigeons that were concealed in five boxes positioned 20 yards or so in front of the shooter. When the shooter called 'Pull', a wire linked to any one of the five boxes was pulled, opening the box or trap and releasing the pigeon.

Large sums of money would be wagered on the outcome of such shooting, and even up until the 1960s places like Monte Carlo were famous for their live pigeon events. Live pigeon shooting disappeared from the UK when Queen Victoria allegedly disapproved. The late Princess Grace of Monaco, formerly actress Grace Kelly, put a stop to the game in Monte Carlo.

Trap shooting using clay targets retains much of the form of the old live pigeon shooting. The targets still start out in front of the shooter and go away at a variety of angles and heights. All trap shooting of any consequence is done with the gun already mounted in the shoulder, live pigeon style, although nowadays the only suffering caused is to the shooters' pockets, especially those who favour the international disciplines, which can be quite expensive.

Clay shooting is a marvellous sport at all levels, and even those who are confined to a wheelchair can attain a level of skill that would be impossible in many other sports. It is a sport for everybody.

Equipment

Selecting a gun

Selecting the right gun for your discipline is a very important step. A mistake here will compromise your shooting and frustrate your efforts to improve.

Over the years guns for the individual disciplines have taken on a very definite persona, to the point that a purpose-built Trap gun, for instance, is little use in its unmodified form for Sporting and quite hopeless for Skeet. The days of the one-gun-for-everything idea have long departed for those who take their shooting seriously.

Multi-chokes have helped eliminate the distinctions to a limited degree, but simply screwing two full-choke tubes into a Sporting gun will not necessarily make it the idea tool for Trap. Elements of weight, balance and stock dimensions all play their part, too, and these are not readily altered.

When talking about guns for clay shooting you are talking about guns

Trap stock (top) and Skeet stock

9

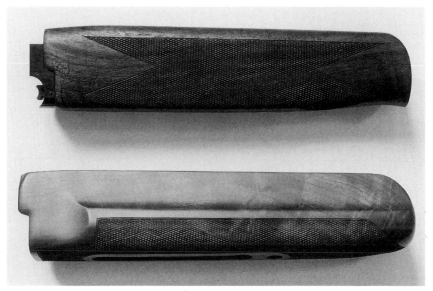

Schnabel type fore-end (top) and standard type fore-end

with a single sighting plane, that is, over-and-unders and semi-automatics. Pump guns are allowed but are rarely seen outside the USA, and even then their use tends to be confined to single barrel Trap events. I have a certain regard for pump guns, and have used them very effectively, but not for clay shooting!

In some major Sporting competitions there are often side-by-side classes, mainly for those game shooters who wish to try their luck at clay shooting. The scores achieved rarely come close to the winning score, though, and it's notable that even when top clay shooters use these guns their scores generally fall greatly. Side-by-side guns still have an important place in shooting, but not in clay shooting.

Actions

There are two main action types found on modern over-and-unders. The least common, the sidelock, is expensive, desirable and very pretty, but not strictly necessary if you are interested solely in function. Far more common are clay guns with trigger-plate actions. These tend to be misnamed as boxlocks, to which they bear a close external resemblance, although internally they are quite different.

Sidelock or trigger-plate makes no difference to the target. The important elements have already been mentioned, to which must be added crisp, consistent trigger pulls. Although pull weights of between 3lb and 4lb are generally accepted as right, they must be sharp, too. A good trigger pull has been likened to the snapping of a thin glass rod or icicle. A sloppy or spongy trigger is useless, since it destroys timing, and this is the very essence of good shooting.

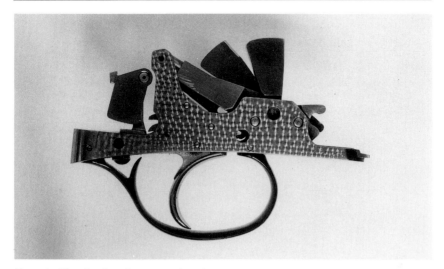

Detachable single trigger mechanism

So keen are some leading clay shooting instructors on correct triggering habits that they get their pupils to shoot whole rounds of Skeet and Trap with just snap caps. There is nothing better to highlight poor trigger pulling habits.

While on the subject of triggers there are some makes that specialise in detachable trigger units. These enable instant access to the trigger mechanism, since the entire unit can be removed from the action, usually by pushing a button or pushing the safety catch forward beyond its normal travel. This latter is the method favoured by Perazzi of Italy, the manufacturers best known for this feature. Others who have this detachable trigger system are Gamba and Beretta, although only on certain guns.

The advantage of instant access is that a spare trigger can be quickly slotted into place should the original go wrong. The disadvantage is that these units are not cheap, and are only found on expensive guns.

Barrels

Barrels come in lengths as short as 25 inches and as long as 34 inches. These two extremes are not available on clay guns in the UK except by special order. Barrel length and related disciplines are discussed further later in the book.

There are a number of features that may be found on the barrels of certain manufacturers, and some that may be included by independent gunsmiths. Barrel porting is very popular in the USA, especially for Sporting guns. Correctly done the porting reduces both recoil and barrel flip, the latter occurring whenever a gun is fired. If it is extreme then the gun goes out of control, and it becomes difficult to bring the barrels quickly onto a second target. Few shooters in the UK have ever noticed

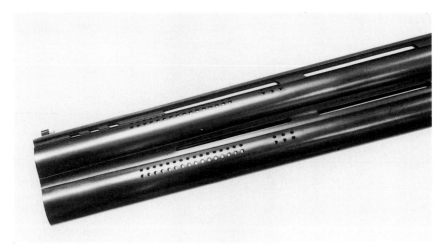

Ported barrels

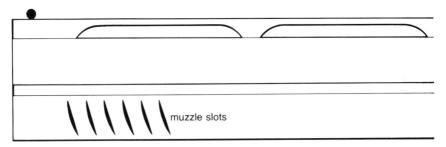

muzzle slots

Barrel porting. Muzzle slots direct gases upwards and backwards, reducing recoil and muzzle flip. They are often only on the lower barrel, as this is fired first. Muzzle flip when the second shot is fired is not important

this being a problem at Sporting, although many Trap shooters have experimented with barrel porting. The porting, which can be holes or slots in the muzzle area, directs the burning gasses backwards and upwards, pushing the barrels in the opposite direction.

The upward thrust counters the tendency of the barrels to kick upwards, and the rearward push cuts down on recoil. However, the slots tend to make the gun much sharper sounding to the shooter and quite unpleasant to anyone standing nearby.

Another idea being pursued in the USA is the lengthening of forcing cones. Forcing cones are what the shot charge must travel through when passing from the cartridge case into the barrel. A sudden narrowing of the forcing cone causes greater back pressure than does an elongated cone, and recoil can be correspondingly greater. Lengthening the cone has the opposite effect, although care has to be exercised to ensure that this isn't overdone. If it is then the gun can be transformed into something that

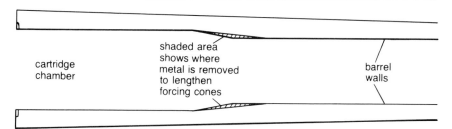

cartridge
chamber

shaded area
shows where
metal is removed
to lengthen
forcing cones

barrel
walls

Lengthening forcing cones

loses all its shooting performance, and it cannot be corrected. American shooters favour the idea, and if it is done properly it will reduce recoil and also tighten patterns. The latter is caused by pressure reduction, and with this goes a slight reduction in velocities, too. There are pros and cons for both barrel porting and cone lengthening, but I doubt these ideas will catch on among conservative shooters in the UK.

Ribs

There is no such thing as an ideal width or type of rib since great shooting has been achieved from very narrow to very wide ribs. Most guns intended for competition use have ventilated ribs as an aid to cooling, and some guns also have ventilated side ribs for the same reason. These features might not seem of great importance until you shoot on a hot day, when heat haze above the rib can cause all sorts of visibility problems.

In shape there is little to beat the typical Browning centre channel style rib, or the Beretta style flat matted variety. Both are mid-width, very pointable, and neat. Most other manufacturers employ similar rib patterns.

The purpose of tapered ribs is to make barrels look longer than they are and thus improve the gun's pointability. The major problem with these ribs is that they are extremely difficult to fit accurately, and many as a result deviate slightly from the dead straight. This makes them far from ideal. You cannot change the rib you have on your gun, so make sure you like the one on the gun you select. If you don't the only solution is to buy another gun.

Balance

Balance is not easy to define, except to say that a gun that is well balanced will feel lively in the hands, yet controllable; it will feel lighter than it is, yet will absorb recoil like a much heavier gun; and it will be comfortable to shoot and will actually make you want to shoot it!

A badly balanced gun, on the other hand, will feel awkward, clumsy, heavier than it actually is, may well thump you when you fire it, and certainly won't feel comfortable to shoot. You won't wish to shoot it any more than you have to.

Balance is all about weight distribution, and plays a significant part in the way a gun shoots. Ideally, the weight should fall equally between the two hands, although where the leading hand is actually positioned on the fore-end will affect this distribution. Many Sporting shooters position their hands a long way back, almost to the action, whereas many Trap shooters have their hands much further forward than this.

Generally speaking, the further forward you place your hand, the slower you will move the gun but you will gain greater muzzle control, and obviously the opposite applies. Trap requires far less realignment of the gun once it has been set on line, while Sporting requires quite abrupt changes of direction.

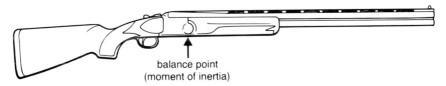

balance point
(moment of inertia)

Balance point

The balance point on a gun, or moment of inertia, is usually thought to be properly situated at the barrel pivot point, on the cross or hinge pin.

Using this guide most guns, particularly those equipped with multi-chokes, tend to be a bit barrel heavy. Of the two extremes, this is the more favourable. A stock heavy gun will move all over the sky without much prompting, and is difficult to control.

If you are a beginner then you won't know a well balanced gun from a badly balanced one. After shooting for a year or two you will have a very sound idea of what a good gun feels like, even if you cannot put that feeling into words. Then try a dozen or more guns from the rack, discard the ones you don't like and perhaps toy with the one you do.

Unfortunately, there is no such thing as 'swing weight' as there is in golf, where each set of clubs is marked according to how it reacts to a certain swing. These golfing classifications are not exactly scientific, but they are a lot better than nothing. Perhaps swing weights are an idea worth following up. If it were possible to devise a method whereby guns could be designated like this, then shooters could ignore those guns that didn't suit their method of shooting and concentrate on the guns that did. It would save a lot of time but probably spoil a lot of the fun, too.

Semi-automatics

The semi-automatic has an important part to play in clay shooting, and guns like the Remington 1100, the 11–87, and the Beretta 303, have found a keen market among shooters who prefer the almost negligible recoil of these guns. There are models available for all three main disciplines. In the

Remington semi-automatic

UK they have found favour in Skeet and Sporting, and have achieved considerable success in these disciplines.

If there is a drawback to semi-automatics it is one of dubious reliability, although this is nothing like the problem it once was. Even so, many who shoot seriously will carry a brace of autos, just in case!

Guns for disciplines

In the right hands any shotgun will make a reasonable job of the targets of any discipline, regardless of whether it is shot at Trap, Skeet or Sporting. However, if you are after perfection, or as near as you can get, this means specialisation.

Sporting

The Sporting gun must be able to handle targets as close as those encountered on a Skeet field, typical medium range targets, and long range targets sometimes further away than anything ever shot on an Olympic Trap field. Because any combination of targets is possible, the Sporting gun must be capable of quick changes of direction and speed while at the same time retaining stability and controllability. Of course, it is the shooter who must actually do all these things, but whereas some guns will hinder his best efforts others will make his job simpler.

Weight

Talking about an ideal weight for a Sporting gun is meaningless unless it is related to the shooter in question. An ideal weight for a big, strong man will be quite different from the ideal weight for a boy or small woman. Sporting guns can be as light as 7 lb or as heavy as 8½ lb.

With the advent of 28 gm ammunition, with its attendant lighter recoil, seven-pound guns are now a sensible choice for smaller shooters, who will find them much easier to push around the sky than they will one of the heavyweights. But what is wanted is a good controllable weight, and

15

while a light gun will be ideally suited to the smaller shooter it will be difficult to control for someone bigger and stronger.

8 lb is as heavy as most people will handle with ease. It is worth bearing in mind that A.J. Smith, a strong man by any standards, shoots tremendous scores with a gun weighing little more than 7½ lb.

Barrel length

It must seem strange to those who have been shooting for many years to see how fashions have changed time and again. In the 'sixties it became fashionable to shoot with relatively short barrels, and 28-inch barrels were thought to be the longest worthy of consideration. Old-fashioned 30-inch barrels were quite definitely out.

Now, 28-inch barrels are thought to be the very shortest worth considering. Many shooters consider 30-inch barrels to be standard fare for Sporting, and an increasing number are taking to guns with 32-inch barrels.

Generally speaking long barrels give greater pointability and control on long targets, but compromise the shooter on closer targets, where making the necessary rapid directional changes becomes more difficult. For the average Sporting shooter 28-inch barrels are adequate. Top shooters, such as John Bidwell who shoots a 27½-inch barrel Browning, have shown that those extra few inches are not really necessary. Many other leading Sporting men shoot very well with 32-inch barrels and so have created the desire in others to follow their example.

Admittedly those racy 32-inch barrelled guns look good, but without the skill, the desire, and the determination to get those long tubes on the target you might as well be using a cork gun. Great shooting doesn't just need big guns: it needs cool nerve and ability.

My feeling is that for every shooter who benefits from 32-inch barrels there are five more who find themselves overgunned. Buy one if you want to be fashionable, but if you are more interested in your score then go for something shorter.

Chokes

Many Sporting guns these days come equipped with multi-chokes, which allow the shooter to swap chokes at each stand if he so chooses (and if the rules allow). There has been a tendency among some shooters to rely on open chokes, such as Improved Cylinder. This gives an admittedly wide pattern but at long range, particularly when you encounter midis or, worse still, minis, there is the chance you won't get any pellets on the target at all.

There is sense in deciding on your chokes and sticking with them, say ¼ in the lower barrel and ½ in the top, and this combination should work well at almost any range and on any target. If you have a multi-choke gun, and don't mind the brief bit of fiddling about required, then get the most out of your gun by suiting the chokes to the shooting stand you are on.

Stocks

Actual dimensions and how to achieve them are closely examined in the chapter on gun fit. An extra for Sporting is the type of butt plate fitted. The black fibre plate fitted to many guns has the disadvantage that it can easily slip in the shoulder as the gun is fired, making a hurried remount necessary instead of a controlled one. An increasing number of manufacturers are fitting thin rubber non-slip pads that work very well. Having your fibre pad changed for a rubber one is relatively cheap and well worth doing.

Trap

These are the most specialised of the guns for the various disciplines. Whereas 28-inch barrels work well for Sporting they are definitely on the short side for Trap. The reason is simple: there are no abrupt changes of direction when shooting Trap, and so control and pointability are essential. 30-inch barrels are standard equipment, while many shooters prefer the extra control of 32-inch barrels.

With shot loads restricted to one ounce, or 28 gm, recoil is no longer a major factor, and it is possible now to shoot a relatively lightweight Trap gun without feeling uncomfortable. This is good for those who wish to shoot long barrelled guns but don't want the weight penalty.

Beretta model ASE90 Trap gun

Typical single trigger action

Chokes

What you decide upon depends on your Trap discipline. If the gun is a multi-choke you can fit ½ and ¾ for Down-The-Line (most people will prefer more); and ¾ and Full; or Full and Full, for the international Trap disciplines. It's well worthwhile patterning your gun with its various chokes just to see how it performs with your favoured brand of ammunition. Some brands shoot tighter than others and this will be affected to some extent by the ammunition you shoot. Some types will shoot much tighter patterns through a given choke than others, and you won't know which is which unless you carry out pattern tests.

Screwing in a multichoke tube

Stocks

Most Trap shooters prefer their guns to shoot a touch on the high side, although in recent years this has been taken to extremes by some of the leading shooters.

The purpose of this high stock is to allow the shooter to shoot right at even the high rising targets of international Trap disciplines, without having consciously to lead them by shooting over the top of them. The disadvantage of this is when a very low target sneaks out. The high stock users argue that they soon learn to compensate and their results prove that they do, too.

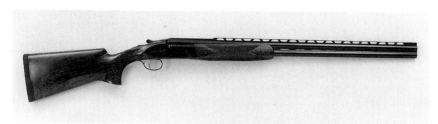

Special stepped rib on a Perazzi MX8 Trap gun

28-inch and 30-inch barrels on a pair of Classic Doubles guns

Skeet

A Skeet gun has to perform several functions. It has to shoot fairly flat, needing nothing like the high stock of the Trap gun. It also needs to throw a wide pattern, since the targets are no more than 20 yards or so away at the most, and sometimes they are as near as 7 to 8 yards.

Many shooters these days make their Sporting gun double as a Skeet gun. With the advent of multi-chokes this is eminently sensible, at least for domestic Skeet. There is no difference between a Sporting gun and a domestic Skeet gun except in the chokes, where most Skeet shooters will opt for cylinder in both barrels.

Some Skeet shooters happily shoot much tighter chokes than this, and there is no arguing that they sometimes achieve winning scores. But with all Skeet targets being relatively close range any degree of choke makes greater demands on accuracy.

For ISU Skeet things aren't quite so easy. On these faster targets no one shoots with barrels longer than 28 inches. Anything longer will make the doubles very difficult. There is also less room for error, and so as wide a pattern as possible, consistent with good breaks, is the order of the day, even though shot loads have been reduced to 28 gm. For this discipline a cylinder choke will do the job, and retro choke are even better.

Stocks

A Sporting gun will work well on domestic Skeet but for ISU the stock wants to shoot higher, more like a Trap than a Skeet gun. The reason for this lies in the ISU Skeet ready position, with the stock on the hip. However well you mount the gun there is no getting away from the fact that as the stock is being brought to the shoulder the muzzles are going to dip slightly. This is not the violent see-saw motion of the poor shot, but the gun will tend to shoot low even in the best hands unless some form of compensation is built in.

My own ISU Skeet gun has a stock similar in height to a DTL Trap gun. From the ISU ready position it shoots just about dead on. Sadly it shoots too high for English Skeet!

Which make?

There are many makes of gun on the market, and generally speaking the better the gun the more it is going to cost. Which make to go for is a matter of opinion. Each major manufacturer has keen followers, and all have their shooters who have won major events worldwide.

It is very difficult to decide on a particular make since they all have something going for them. If you are a complete novice then you should explain to the gun shop how much you are prepared to spend, tell them what you will be using the gun for and then take their advice. If you tell them that you want a gun suitable for all disciplines and that you have £150 to spend don't be surprised if they can't help you!

Look to spend at least £400 on a new gun, perhaps £100 less on a similar second-hand model, and even then regard that as a starter gun to see you through your first season or two. Once you have that under your belt you will have formed a much better idea of what shooting is about and also will have developed firm ideas about guns. Then you can trade up to something better. You can pay a small fortune if your bank account allows it, yet many of the leading shooters use guns costing less than £1,000. Before rushing out to spend lots of hard-earned money, remember that a sound gun that fits is only part of the success equation. It's the person behind it that really counts.

Cartridges

The years have seen a gradual reduction in permissible shot loads across nearly all the disciplines. The main reason for this is a desire on the part of the ISU and, to a lesser extent, FITASC, to reduce recoil and eventually to reduce ammunition costs.

The latter is very unlikely to happen. For many years ammunition costs have been kept artificially low, with manufacturers' margins borderline. Now prices of the new one ounce/28 gm ammunition are starting to go up.

The supposed reduction in recoil is also a moot point. Many manufac-

Cartridge and components

turers have taken advantage of the lighter shot load to push velocities higher than ever, with the result that recoil for many leading competition loads is little different in one ounce guise to what it was when 1⅛ ounce was permitted. There has never been a greater choice of ammunition for all the disciplines. With quality so good, sorting out one or two to suit you, your gun and your pocket is not that difficult.

Recoil should be a major factor in your search for the ideal ammunition. The perfect cartridge would have none, combined with high velocity. Unfortunately, physics doesn't work that way. The higher the velocity, the more the apparent recoil is likely to be, and if you notice recoil every time you fire your gun then you are being distracted. If you start to bruise as a result, then you will soon be so distracted you won't want to shoot, and if you do continue you will hit very little.

So a sweet shooting cartridge is far more important than one that just has sheer speed to recommend it. It's worthwhile testing yourself and your gun with a variety of ammunition types and makes, forgetting about advertised velocities. A few feet per second one way or the other won't make any difference anyway, but an uncomfortable cartridge soon will.

Sporting

Any target in range (and some not in range) qualifies as a Sporting target, and there is a sound argument for carrying several shot sizes to handle the targets on different stands. But there is another school of thought that advocates one shot size for everything. Personally, I am sure that a shooter armed with a good cartridge loaded with 7½ shot (Italian 8 shot) will never miss because of his ammunition. 9s will break close targets; 8s will handle close and mid-range targets; 7½s will handle the lot.

Trap

For DTL any good cartridge will do the job well, and either 8s or 7½s will handle any DTL target. For the international disciplines there are many loads, some intended as 'first barrel' loads, others as 'second barrel' loads. Needless to say the second barrel ammunition is intended for those long second shots at fast disappearing targets that have already been shot at once, and missed. Since these are often at over 38 yards it is essential that the ammunition selected be very consistent and throw first class patterns.

Speed is not essential, and indeed some of the finest second barrel loads are actually somewhat slower than those intended for the first barrel. At long range, granted reasonable velocity, pattern is all.

As to whether you should opt for plated ammunition, that is up to you. It used to be thought that nickel plating meant tighter patterns, but this is not always true. Certain makes of cartridge shoot their tightest patterns with hardened shot having a high antimony content. Although you can pattern test your ammunition you will probably learn as much from the feedback you get when actually shooting and breaking targets.

Skeet

9s are the biggest shot size allowed here. But within this limitation there are all sorts of cartridge, some fast, some medium speed and some slow. Generally speaking, the faster you throw lead from a gun the wider the pattern tends to be, and while this can be a disadvantage at other disciplines it can be an advantage at Skeet. But you can overdo the speed aspect.

Some years ago Hull Cartridge Company, who for most of my shooting career sponsored me with both their own excellent ammunition and Fiocchi cartridges, loaded me some 'specials' that were so fast they broke the target almost before I pulled the trigger! The trouble was they also knocked loose one of my front teeth.

You must never forget that at Skeet you are called upon to shoot doubles in quick succession, and in the same plane. A cartridge that kicks the muzzles upwards every time you fire is a positive disadvantage: medium fast and smooth is what you want.

Discovering a cartridge you like is important, and more important is that you then stick with it and don't jump from one brand to another. Even the cheapest cartridges these days have enough performance in them to shoot a good score.

Clothing

There is more to shooting than just buying a gun. You will need a shooting jacket, ear protection, proper shooting glasses, decent shoes, a hat if you wear one and a fair amount of other paraphernalia, too.

How you look and how you feel about yourself make a significant contribution to how you perform. Imagine yourself at a smart dinner party where, knowing nobody and having misread the invitation, you have somehow managed to turn up dressed in jeans and a T-shirt while everyone else is wearing a dinner jacket and black tie. You would have to be a very confident individual indeed not to feel totally out of place and not to be reduced to feeling somewhat inferior to the rest of the gathering.

The same rule applies when you are clay shooting. A smart appearance is very important. You feel part of the scene and this helps your confidence. You won't do yourself any good at all if you look too scruffy.

Jackets

A smart jacket is important but it must also be functional. There are many makes available and it is advisable to try several before buying. Those with short shoulder pads are really only suitable for Trap shooting and not much good for any discipline where you must mount the gun during the shot. It is all too easy for the stock to snag on the pad as the gun is being mounted, and a poor gun mount probably means a missed target.

The best type of jacket for the gun down disciplines will have a full length pad, usually leather, running from the shoulder down to the pocket. Ideally, this will be stitched down its length at one-inch intervals. This prevents the pad from bunching up and snagging the stock. This type of jacket should allow a smooth gun mount, although it needs to be a good fit if it is to do its job properly.

Some shooters prefer to shoot without a jacket, and many ISU Skeet shooters, notably those from eastern Europe, shoot in T-shirts emblazoned with their national emblems. You need to have a cartridge pouch on a belt if you choose just a shirt. The advantage is that gun mounting is made much easier, and most people are amazed at how their gun mounting improves without a shooting jacket. The disadvantage is that recoil can become a little too obvious to those who are susceptible to it.

Another drawback for T-shirt shooters occurs when the cold weather arrives. Slipping on a thin sweater will keep all but the coldest days at bay, by which time most shooters will be looking to hibernate for a month or two anyway!

Shooting glasses

Plain common sense dictates that shooters should wear some form of eye protection, although it's a fact that very few do. Sporting shooters are very prone to injury from clays, mainly broken bits that can go off in all sorts of unexpected directions. Clay targets and their pieces are invariably spinning very quickly, and have sharp edges. If they hit you on an exposed part, then a cut, sometimes deep, is inevitable.

A large piece of clay looped over a protective fence and hit me square in the eye one day when I was shooting Skeet. The impact was sufficient to shatter one lens of my shooting glasses. Had I not been wearing glasses that day then my shooting career would have ended right there.

There is far more to shooting glasses than just eye protection. Good glasses, by which I also mean expensive glasses, are optically corrected and don't cause vision distortion in the way that many 'sunglasses' can. They are also available in a variety of lens tints to suit light conditions as well as to enhance target colours.

This latter is an area that few shooters in the UK have investigated. Most wear dark glasses against the sun and that's all they bother with. But there are also special tints available to deal with awkward backgrounds and target colours.

For several years I struggled whenever I was forced to shoot orange 'blaze' targets. They are almost impossible to see in certain light conditions. The problem is that they are too bright and pale. If the sun is on them and they are against the sky, most shooters will find them a tricky proposition.

The cure is an appropriate lens colour. My glasses have interchangeable lenses, and whenever I encounter 'blaze' targets I wear bronze tinted ones. Their effect is to reduce the brightness of the targets and also to make them appear a deeper red. This makes them contrast more with a light background, so that they stand out better, without making them difficult to see against a dark background. I like to wear this lens colour for most targets these days, and will only use dark grey or green lenses when looking towards the sun.

There are many other lens colours available. Yellow is widely recommended when the light is poor, although as any photography enthusiast will tell you there is no such thing as a filter colour that increases available light. Those who possess a light meter, or a camera equipped with an inbuilt metering system, can prove this point for themselves simply by holding a yellow lens in front of the meter and watching the reaction: about one F-stop of light is absorbed. In bad light you want as much light to reach the eye as is available, and this means wearing no glasses at all or completely plain glass lenses. For safety reasons the latter is the obvious choice.

Other colours that have found favour over the years are various shades of red, several bronze tints, greens, greys, yellows and even orange. In my own shooting bag I have dark bronze, light bronze, dark green and clear. I dislike red, find no use for yellow and prefer green to grey when direct sunlight is causing problems.

While any optically corrected glasses are usable for shooting there are several other features that are important:

(a) the lenses should be broad and fairly deep
(b) the nose clips should be adjustable for height and width
(c) there should be a sweat bar to hold the frame clear of the face
(d) the side frames should curl around the ears to prevent any movement of the glasses during shooting.

If you opt for interchangeable lens type glasses it's always a good idea to have a spare frame with you in case of emergencies.

Side shields

For Skeet shooters there are few things more disconcerting than having someone come into their vision as they prepare to call for a target. This is inexcusable; no member of the squad should be allowed to wander into a shooter's eyeline. It happens often enough on peg five, if you happen to be number six on the squad, and far too many times on peg six, where the ignorant will walk round almost to the low house. The answer really lies with firm refereeing, a short sharp remark from the offended shooter, or wearing eye shields. These are easily made from cardboard and attach to the sideframes of your glasses.

Trap shooters, especially those who shoot international disciplines, have to endure lots of other shooter movement, and eye shields are worn by many to overcome the problem.

Ear protection

When I first became involved with firearms hardly any shooters wore any form of ear protection. Because of this many older shooting men are now either totally deaf or nearly so. It is significant that in a recent study of people who have lost their senses of sight and hearing, the large majority, given the choice of regaining one or the other, said they would prefer to have back their sense of hearing. Protecting your hearing is vital!

This is the most important and obvious reason for wearing some form of hearing protection. But there are others, too, related to shooting performance. The energy sapping effect of noise is well known, and if your own 100 or so shots in a day are unlikely to cause too many problems, then consider the effect of all the other thousands of bangs going on around you. Look at a typical round of Olympic Trap as an example. Six shooters shoot at 25 targets each: 150 targets. But even if all six are really shooting well it is likely that those 150 targets are going to require 200 shots. In a four round competition this means that each shooter is directly exposed to 800 loud bangs. Taking account also of the refereeing time required during that day, again meaning direct exposure to shooting, the average Olympic Trap shooter in a typical 100 target shoot will be directly exposed to around 1,200 shots. A Sporting shooter at a big event will have to endure even more.

Apart from the certain permanent damage to hearing following sustained exposure of this kind, the effect on the nerves and on the ability to concentrate is considerable. So some form of hearing protection is vital to good shooting performance.

It has been shown that no form of wearable hearing protection is totally effective. If it is possible to shoot in it then the system is not 100% perfect. Ear muffs are far more effective than ear plugs, and both combined are even better.

The problem most people experience with ear muffs is one of being cut off from the rest of the world, probably a very similar feeling to that suffered by those who are deaf. Wearing them takes a certain period of familiarisation, and I freely admit that muffs are something I never liked or have ever got used to. Probably wrongly, I prefer good ear plugs.

The latest types of electronic ear muff, which permit only low level sound to reach the wearer, overcome many of the objections of being cut off. The best ones have a volume control so that you can hear normal conversation but gunfire is automatically blocked. When you want to cut out everything and everybody you just turn down the volume control and disappear into your own silent world!

Hats

Many shooters never shoot in hats, others always do. The peaked variety may afford some shade fron frontal sunlight, though I doubt it, whereas big hats can possibly keep off the sun.

Truly functional hats either keep off the sun or they protect the shooter against cold or rain. Sun hats are essential in hot countries, and anyone who has ever tried to think straight in temperatures of 100°F will know the impossibility of performing even the most mediocre task without protection from a baleful sun. A white cotton hat with a floppy rim is much favoured, and if it is drenched in water immediately prior to a round in scorching temperatures then as the moisture evaporates it will take away a lot of heat from your head, too.

Bad weather and how to handle it

There is an art to surviving a shoot in bad weather, and it's not just a case of pulling on the waterproof outfit. Your shooting is bound to suffer if:

(a) you get thoroughly wet and chilled
(b) your gun becomes wet and slippery
(c) you cannot see properly
(d) your hands get so cold they lose sensitivity
(e) you lose interest and wish to go home.

Point (e) is bound to arise if you suffer from (a), (b), (c) and (d). There is no need to put up with any of them. Although you can never totally eliminate their effects you can at least reduce them to tolerable levels.

The following are items you should always carry to every shoot:

(a) thin golf-type waterproofs made of really waterproof materials: expensive but worth every penny. Strange though it may sound the shooting jacket should be worn on top
(b) a good hat
(c) several hand towels
(d) a large umbrella
(e) a complete change of clothes in case you get caught in a real downpour
(f) a serious waterproof jacket, such as a Barbour, that can be worn over the shoulders between stations or between stands.

If it looks as though it's going to rain, then put on the golf suit. It's too late to put it on later when you are already soaked. Wear a towel around your neck to stop water getting in, and carry another towel with you to dry the gun and your hands between stands. Wet hands soon get cold, and it's amazing the difference a towel can make. Some sort of hat is essential in rain, or you will soon look and feel like a drowned rat.

An umbrella is perfect to hide under between stands. You are actually only called upon to shoot for a minute or two; in between times a Barbour jacket or similar can take the brunt of the rain and keep you warmer and drier than the golf suit can on its own.

When confronted with driving rain most people automatically pull off their shooting glasses, whereas they ought to be putting them on. Water running down the lens might be a distraction but far less so than are eyes full of driven rain. It's better to see a bit than to see nothing at all.

Shooting well in rotten weather is as much an act of will power as it is of appropriate clothing, although you need both. Keep your ears open when the weather closes in and you will hear 75% of the opposition talk themselves out of contention. Maintain a positive attitude yourself and you've already beaten these people. Dress sensibly, and regard bad weather as just another challenge to be faced and overcome.

Shoes

Most serious shooters these days wear some form of training shoes, and these are so much better than the odd assortment of footwear that once adorned clay shooting areas. Working boots, wellingtons, open-toed sandals, etc. have no place on the clay shooting field, although wellingtons are acceptable at a Sporting shoot where you might be wading through mud and water. For Skeet and Sporting, though, they look very unprofessional. In the wet, wear waterproof shoes by all means, or cleated walking shoes.

Leather soled shoes can prove a very bad idea on certain surfaces, and anyone who has ever tried to wear these shoes on a smooth wet shooting stand will know what I mean. There are some shooters who like to wear brogues, and very smart they are, too. But if you decide to wear them get some rubber soles on them before you take them to a shoot.

Bag fillers

Dipping into my own shooting bag I find the following items over and above those already mentioned that have accompanied me around the world many times. They include: cartridge extractor, snap caps, gun oil, spare springs and strikers for the gun, a complete trigger mechanism, a tube of Superglue for instant repairs, a small sewing kit, spare shoe laces, several hats, gun cleaning kit, pens and paper, safety pins, screwdriver, socket spanner for removing stock, a small tool kit, paper handkerchiefs and glasses cleaning cloth.

Many of the items are probably the result of a pessimistic outlook. I have never needed the spare triggers. Some were in use all the time — gun oil, sewing kit, hats, handkerchiefs. There are other things that could be added and some that could be left at home. You will soon fill your bag with your own items. I only hope they travel as far and as frequently as mine have.

Gun fit

Gun fit has long been recognised as an essential ingredient of good shooting, but despite this few shooters pay any attention to it beyond perhaps discussing its virtues with others of like mind. Doing something about it is usually another matter entirely.

The problem with gun fit is that there are almost as many ideas as to what it might or might not be as there are shooters. One thing is certain: while a well fitted gun will feel comfortable to use, it is possible to have a gun that feels very comfortable to use but that is not a good fit.

A well fitted gun can be likened to any other item of sports equipment that is matched to its owner. A top shooter will take as much trouble over his gun as will a Test cricketer over his cricket bat, an international tennis player over his rackets, or a top professional golfer over his golf clubs. Each knows that the right equipment will enhance his ability to play the game well.

A well fitted gun performs just one all-important function. It ensures that when the gun is mounted correctly it will point exactly to the spot on which the shooter is concentrating his attention. What good gun fit will not do, and never can, is compensate for poor style, bad technique or simple lack of ability.

For these reasons, a well fitted gun will be of more benefit to the good experienced shot than to the newcomer or occasional shooter. Indeed, to try to achieve an exact gun fit for someone who has not developed proper style and form is very difficult and perhaps a waste of time. The following is an example as to why this is so. A man standing square to his target will need a shorter stock than if he were to adopt a style in which he stood more sideways on. Until a style is developed, therefore, it is premature to attempt an accurate gun fit. Having said that, even a beginner needs a gun that approximates to a decent gun fit rather than one that is a long way out.

There are two ways to achieve a good gun fit. One is to visit a competent shooting school that has try-gun facilities and gun fitters with the skill to use them properly. Not all shooting school instructors have this talent, and many schools have no try-guns either. Even some of the famous schools have only one or two men with the necessary skills to do the job properly.

The other and better way for the competition shooter is to do the job himself. A fair gun fit can be achieved reasonably easily, while with time and application the shooter can adjust his gun until it truly suits his needs exactly.

A try-gun used to illustrate a stock that is too long   *A stock that is too short*

The three basic elements of gun fit are as follows:

(a) the length of the stock, measured from the trigger to the centre of the butt

(b) the height of the stock, known as the bend or the drop, which is measured by extending a line from the rib and then measuring the perpendicular from this line to various points on the comb of the stock

(c) the cast, which refers to the degree of offset in the stock when viewed from the rear.

The accompanying illustrations will help explain these measurements more clearly.

The functions of the dimensions

Length

It is easy to understand that an extremely long stock will be difficult to cope with. It will make smooth gun mounting almost impossible and will

Stock length here is about right

force the shooter to position his leading hand too far back on the gun. In extreme cases this hand will be back on the action. A very short stock will make the gun difficult to control as well as uncomfortable to shoot. The leading hand will be positioned too far forwards on the gun, often out on the barrels and beyond the fore-end. There is an optimum length of stock for every shooter.

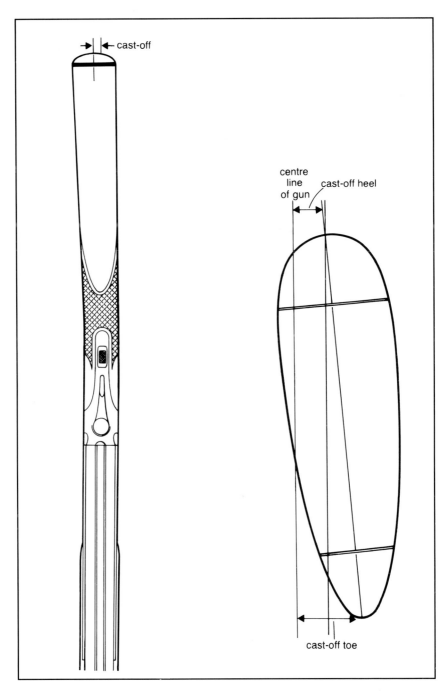

cast-off

centre
line
of gun

cast-off heel

cast-off toe

Gun fit (top view) – cast-off

Gun fit (rear view of stock). Greater cast-off at the toe allows the gun to sit in the shoulder properly and prevents canting

32

Other length dimensions

Apart from the basic measurement taken from trigger to butt centre there are two other important dimensions. These are the length at heel and the length at toe. The angle at which the butt plate meets the centre length measurement is known as the pitch. On the stocks of many factory standard guns the usual set of stock length measurements finds the length at heel being ⅛ inch longer than that at centre, while the length at toe is ⅜ inch longer. This gives the classic concave sweep to the butt plate which allows it to sit comfortably in the shoulder. Depending on the individual, and to a degree the discipline, this pitch angle can be altered.

Bend or drop

The height of the stock relative to the top rib decides how high the gun points relative to the shooter's eye. A gun with too low a stock, which is said to have too much drop, will tend to shoot below the point on which the shooter is concentrating. A gun with too little drop will tend to shoot above this point. As with stock length, there is an optimum drop measurement for every shooter, although to further complicate the issue this can vary slightly according to the discipline! Generally speaking, a high stock is to be preferred to one which is too low. While it is possible to live with the high stock, the low stock is an impossible thing to shoot with.

Cast

Viewed from the rear, a stock that is set to the right is said to have cast off, whereas a stock set to the left is said to have cast on. Generally speaking, the latter is for left handed shooters while the former is for those who are right handed. However, this is not always the case. Although cast can be used to compensate for an eye problem by game shooters with side-by-side guns, this is seldom resorted to by clay shooters who invariably use over-and-unders. I have seen side-by-side guns with sufficient cast-off to allow the left eye to see exactly over the centre of the rib while the stock is mounted in the right shoulder. The result of this extreme example of cast-off, known as an across-eyed stock, is unattractive to say the least.

Over-and-under guns, possibly because of their slimmer profile as presented to the shooter's eye, seldom require much cast off or on to compensate for eye problems. Shooters who need an inch or more cast when using a side-by-side gun are often pleasantly surprised to find that they need hardly any when they change to an over-and-under.

For most clay shooters cast is built into a gun so that with the gun properly mounted the shooter's leading eye aligns exactly over the centre of the top rib. Depending on an individual's facial and physical shape this can mean anything from a completely straight stock, lacking any cast at all, to a stock with as much as half an inch of cast off or on.

Cast is not necessarily confined to the comb of the stock. Frequently, the cast measured at the toe is greater than that at the face or heel. This feature will prevent ladies and muscular men being hit in the chest by the toe of the stock. Often, especially where ladies are concerned, the stock can be made even more comfortable by radiusing the toe of the stock to get rid of the sharp edge.

It would be very nice if gun fit could be determined by a person's height and arm length. All that would be necessary would be to take the measurements, consult a chart and the job would be done. It isn't that simple, unfortunately. A strong muscular shooter will tend to need a shorter stock than a slim person of the same height. If he has a short squat neck then he will probably require a higher stock than his slim counterpart with a long neck. Similarly, if at all full in the face, he might need more cast-off than the slim man. Each individual has his or her ideal gun dimensions. Finding them is easier than you might think.

Discovering the master eye

Before any attempt at gun fit can be made you must find which of your eyes is the master. When using a gun you can obviously see better with two eyes open than with one of them shut. If you are right handed, which means you will naturally hold the gun with your left hand forward and your right pulling the trigger, the stock of the gun will sit against the right side of your face, immediately under your right eye. If the gun is to align exactly on the target then it is essential that the right eye is entirely in charge. In other words it is the master eye and all alignment is done by it exclusively. If your left eye has a say in where the gun points, then it will cause the gun to point to the left of the target. In extreme cases, where the left eye is actually the master, the gun can point as much as three or four feet to the left of a target at 40 yards.

It must be remembered that this misalignment is entirely unconscious from the shooter's point of view, and as far as he is concerned he is pointing the gun straight at the target. The shooter with this problem will miss frequently, but he will be unaware of the reason unless it is demonstrated. Here is how to test yourself for eye dominance.

All that is needed is a four inch square of cardboard with a one inch round hole in the centre. Hold the card in one hand and select a mark in the distance. Keeping both eyes open, raise the card so that it comes between the eyes and the mark. You will be able to see the mark through the hole, but only with one of your two eyes. By shutting an eye you will soon see which it is that is seeing the mark through the hole. This is the dominant eye.

But this test doesn't show that one eye is totally dominant, only that it is the one with which the gun will more readily align. If you find that, as a right hander, your left eye is the dominant one then there is one course of action – shoot with the left eye closed. It is possible to learn to shoot from the left shoulder but it will feel quite unnatural even if you have

The effect of a left master eye

Closing the left eye to correct a sighting error

never held a gun in your life before. In my opinion it is not worth the effort. Many champions shoot with an eye closed, so take the easy route and follow their example.

Should you find that the right eye is the dominant one then you can take the next step. This is to shoot at a fixed mark at about 30 yards, with both eyes open. This needs to be done several times to eliminate any bad shots. It is essential that these shots are taken without conscious aim, or the result is meaningless. If all is well then the shots will all be straight with no tendency to go left. At this stage the elevation of the shots doesn't matter.

If the shots do align to the left, perhaps just catching the mark with the edge of the pattern, then seriously consider closing an eye for future shooting. If the misalignment is a matter of just a few inches, then this can be corrected by adjusting the cast, which will be dealt with later in this chapter.

Finding your stock length

This is always the first measurement to sort out, because it can affect the amount of cast and drop that is needed. A good rule of thumb, that will identify the stock length you need to within ¼ inch or so, is to bend the right arm to a right angle and to place the stock in the bend of the arm thus formed. If the trigger finger can barely reach the trigger then the stock is too long. If it curls very easily around the trigger, and can perhaps reach the front of the trigger guard, then the stock is too short. Ideally the first joint of the trigger finger will comfortably reach the trigger without stretching or over-reaching.

If the stock is too long, you can remove the butt plate or recoil pad. This will shorten the stock from a ¼ inch to as much as an inch. Now

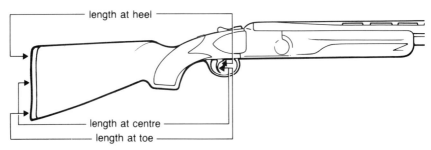

Gun fit (side view) – stock length

try the length test again. If you are in luck then the stock will now be too short, and by taping thicknesses of card in place of the butt plate the ideal length can be found. Once this is satisfactory the stock length can be properly altered by your local gunshop or you can do it yourself if you feel confident.

If having removed the butt plate the stock is still too long, then you may have to enlist the aid of a gunsmith to help you decide how much needs to be removed. It's quite possible that for small men, or ladies, as much as an inch will have to be removed before the stock is the proper length. Don't worry that you might spoil the look of the gun. No one can shoot with a stock that is ½ inch too long, let alone an inch.

As was mentioned earlier, there is more to stock length than just the centre measurement. For ladies and men with a fuller chest the toe measurement need be no more than an ⅛ inch greater than the centre measurement, instead of the more usual ⅜ inch. It is also more comfortable if the toe is rounded instead of sharp. For Skeet shooters, particularly those who shoot the international version, this measurement will suit anyone better than will the standard dimension.

One of the features of a number of modern guns is the adjustable trigger that can be moved back and forth, giving a length adjustment of some ⅜ inch. These can save a lot of stock hacking.

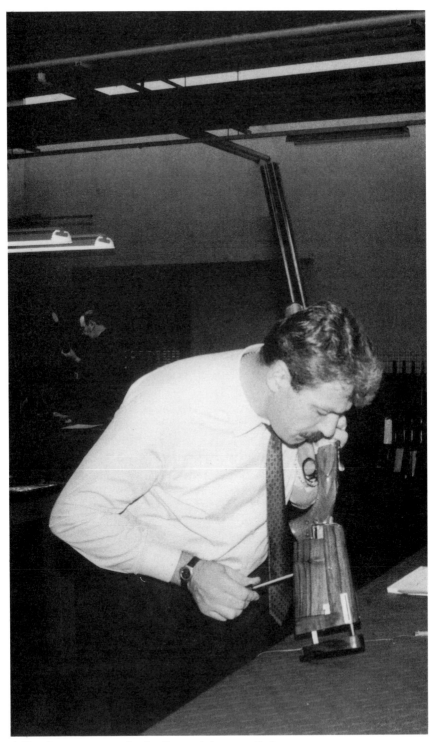

Adjusting a try-gun in the Perazzi factory, Italy

The drop measurement

There has been a growing trend over the past few years to fit competition stocks in such a way that they don't shoot exactly to where the shooter looks but somewhat higher. This has always been the case with many Trap guns, where the shooter is presented with targets that are rising to a greater or lesser degree. The idea of the high stock is that the shooter can concentrate solely on line and let the gun take care of the elevation.

There are sound reasons for having Skeet and Sporting guns that shoot high, too. Observation over the years has shown that far more targets are missed low than are ever missed high. There are limits to this, of course, and nowadays most knowledgeable shooters expect their guns to throw two thirds of their pattern above the mark. This may be readily checked.

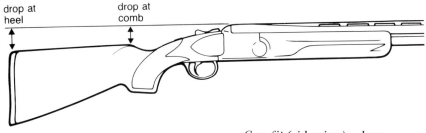

Gun fit (side view) – drop

Aim your shots at a fixed mark and check the results. If the patterns are indeed placed two thirds high, then all is well. More often than not they will be dead centre, however. The easy way to adjust this is to tape thin strips of card to the comb of the stock and retest until the pattern is going where it should. The stock can then be adjusted to suit by your gunsmith. If the gun is shooting too high, then the comb must be carefully cut down until it is shooting in the right place. You can do this yourself, carefully, then let your gunsmith tidy it up.

The cast-off measurement

For most of us this can be left alone, since we already decided that any major misalignment could be cured by closing an eye. If the gun shoots slightly left (no more than six inches off centre) then this can be corrected by sweeping a small amount of wood away from the face of the stock, where the face touches the stock. As little as ⅛ inch will do the job, and once again your gunsmith can do the tidying up.

Of course, anyone handy with tools can do all the work himself, including the re-oiling or refinishing. How to do this is beyond the scope of this book but there are excellent books on the subject. If you have to read about it, though, it might be best to leave the work to an expert.

Finding a discipline

Some disciplines will suit certain shooters more than others. There are those who find themselves drawn to Trap shooting, others to Skeet, and yet another group that favours Sporting. But many shooters find that whereas they might be good ball game players, and do well at squash, tennis or football, they can make nothing whatever of clay shooting. They make little or no progress, and being discouraged may give up. More often than not this is because they have not learned or been taught good technique from the outset. Another reason, however, and far from obvious, is that their temperament and mentality do not match their chosen discipline.

This perhaps surprising statement has been borne out in fact, and was first discovered by a sports psychologist working with rifle and pistol shooters. It had long been suspected that individual shooters might be more naturally attuned to one discipline than another, but proving it and profitting from the knowledge was something else altogether.

Sports psychologists working with competitors at the top level analysed the shooters' various arousal levels, and divided those tested into the two familiar groups, extrovert and introvert. By setting each shooter a number of carefully worded questions, and marking his or her answers with a score, they were able to determine not only who was extrovert or introvert but also to what degree. Those with a score of 100% were the most extrovert, while those with a score of 0% were the most introvert. The results of these tests made it possible to categorise various disciplines by the character of the most successful performers.

Generally speaking, introverts are those who require a very low level of stimulation to cause their hearts to beat faster and for performance-enhancing adrenalin to be released into their system. Extroverts, on the other hand, require a higher level of arousal before they start to get excited. In this way it was discovered that those shooting the prone rifle discipline were the most introverted shooters, while those involved in rapid fire pistol were the most extroverted. In between these extremes were those who shot the many other rifle and pistol disciplines.

By testing other shooters in the same way it was then possible to say that shooter 'A', who for instance shot 50 metre pistol, was actually too extroverted for this discipline and should be shooting rapid fire pistol. Shooter 'B', on the other hand, who was moderately successful as a three positional rifle shooter, might actually do better shooting prone rifle since he was very much an introvert.

A similar test was carried out in the UK on clay shooters, although unfortunately this was only done with a test group of leading Olympic Trap and ISU Skeet shooters. It was discovered that the Trap shooters were middle level introverts, averaging around 35%, while the Skeet shooters were middle level extroverts, averaging around 65%.

Interestingly enough, a number of the individual Trap shooters, who most laymen would nominate as extroverts, were in fact classified from the tests as introverts. Several of the Skeet shooters would have attracted the reverse opinion, but all dropped neatly into the extrovert group.

Anyone familiar with both groups would have no trouble identifying that there is a noticeable difference between groups of leading Trap shooters and groups of leading Skeet shooters. For instance, most ground owners in Great Britain would agree that Skeet shooters are generally a more easy going bunch than Trap shooters, although there are, of course, individual exceptions!

Exactly where top Sporting shooters might slot into these groupings is impossible to say. Remembering that some apparently extrovert types were actually shown in the Trap/Skeet example to be introverts, it would obviously be wrong to make assumptions. The point is this, however. Those who shoot Sporting best will fit into one or other of the categories, and anyone who doesn't belong in that group will be something of a square peg in a round hole. Any shooter who cannot achieve a decent standard at his chosen clay discipline might find it worthwhile to have a go at a different one.

In Czechoslovakia, one of the world's leading shooting countries, newcomers to shooting are introduced to the sport on the prone rifle range. They are taught the all-important basics of shooting, and their progress is carefully monitored. After the initial training stage they are introduced to basic clay shooting. Depending on their obvious leanings and levels of aptitude the newcomers become either Trap or Skeet shooters, but never both!

Few shooters in the West have the patience to learn in this way, nor does the sport have the necessary funds to pay for the sort of individual monitoring required. These setbacks don't prevent individuals from experimenting with the various disciplines, though, and for this reason it would be wrong for newcomers to pick a discipline from the outset and stick with it.

Most people begin their clay shooting careers on a Sporting layout, and because these are far more plentiful than Skeet or Trap layouts, this is the discipline that most shooters stick with. But you don't have to. Try all the disciplines before specialising. Apart from anything else it will give you a more rounded shooting education and at the same time will allow you to find the discipline to which you are best suited. If you can drive a car, catch a ball, and walk without tripping over your feet, you ought to be able to shoot to a decent standard at something!

Basics

While the title of this book is *Competitive Clay Target Shooting*, a chapter explaining the basic methods of shotgun shooting is essential. Studying advanced technique is of little use if the reader's *basic* technique is poor, and to labour on with a method that is basically flawed will lead the shooter nowhere other than perhaps to the psychiatrist's couch. Good shooting is much easier than some people make it appear, but only if basic technique is sound.

Shooting methods

A sound shooting method is one that, without frills, will allow the shooter to hit targets consistently. There are numerous ways of shooting. The professionals who give trick shooting exhibitions prove this. They can shoot targets with guns held upside down, one handed, over shoulders using a mirror and between the legs. Shooting is done at the run, or on a monocycle. Multiple targets are thrown in the air and all are broken before they hit the ground. All this is wonderful to behold, yet the wonder is not just at the marvellous skill of the trick shooters, but at the fact that they manage to hit anything at all when using such strange methods!

A sound shooting method, then, won't have this element of wonder about it. Knowledgeable onlookers will not be pressed to say to their companions, 'How did he do that?', when they watch you shooting. A good shooting method works because it is logical that it should do so, with no trace of magic about it.

All shooting methods have one goal, that is to place the shot charge on the target. With the rare exceptions of those targets that fly exactly at or exactly away from the shooter, with no apparant deviations of line, all targets are either crossing, rising, dropping, curling, or a combination of these. Although the shot charge travels very quickly, at around 1,200 feet per second as it leaves the muzzle, it doesn't arrive at the target the instant that the shooter pulls the trigger. To compensate for this time lag the gun must be pointing ahead of the target as the gun is fired.

Aiming the gun directly at the target doesn't work. In the case of a long range shot, say at a crossing target some 40 yards distant, it is quite possible that the target will have moved on some 15 feet or more by the time the shot arrives. To compensate for this the gun must be pointed this

41

Good ready position for a quartering tower target

much ahead of the target as it is fired. This 'pointing ahead' is known as forward allowance, or shorter and simpler still, lead.

The famous shooting authority and gunmaker, the late Robert Churchill, gave the following analogy to illustrate forward allowance. A country boy, angered by an inconsiderate passing car, picks up a turnip and throws it at the offending vehicle. As Churchill points out, if the boy throws the

Good balance on a crossing target

turnip straight at the car as it passes, the vegetable will drop well behind it. However, if he throws the turnip well in front of the car he might make a demonstration. Churchill had his own ideas about how this forward allowance might be achieved, and there is more of this later in the chapter. Meanwhile, the following are the various accepted ways by which the shooter might throw his own turnip!

43

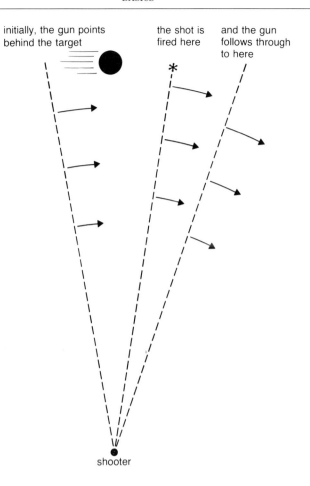

initially, the gun points behind the target

the shot is fired here

and the gun follows through to here

shooter

The swing through method

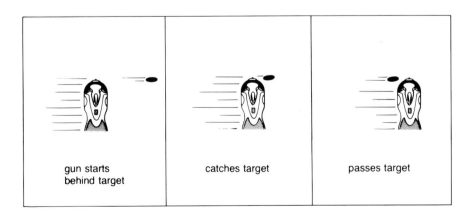

gun starts behind target

catches target

passes target

Swing-through

Swing-through is the most natural of the shooting methods, and probably the most popular, although it is unlikely to be the oldest. It is the traditional game shooting method as well as the one used by all Trap shooters, many Sporting shooters and some Skeet shooters. As the name suggests, the shooter swings the gun through the target. Initially, the shooter points the gun behind the target. He then swings the gun up to and past the target. Done properly, the swing gradually accelerates. The shooter fires after the gun has overtaken the target. How soon after depends upon such factors as target range, its speed and the shooter's personal reaction time. With this method there is a certain degree of automatic lead, caused by the delay between the intention to shoot and the actual pulling of the trigger. On certain close targets this can create the impression that no lead whatsoever was necessary, although this is an illusion.

See The master movement for the correct way to get the whole thing moving.

Point and swing

Point and swing is very similar to the swing-through method. The difference is that the shooter initially points the gun at the target as he is bringing the gun to his shoulder. As the gun is coming to the shoulder so it is pushed ahead of the target, the shot being fired when the amount of forward allowance is judged to be right. As with the swing-through method, the gun is accelerated away from the target as the shot is fired.

One of the advantages of this method over swing-through is that it encourages the shooter to move the gun towards the target as he is mounting it. Swing-through can be made to work, though less efficiently, if the shooter first statically mounts the gun and then swings. The drawback with the point and swing method is that it can prove difficult

Swing through series

shot is fired
when lead is
correct

follows through

The point and swing series

| the gun is placed on the target and initially moves with it | the gun pulls gradually ahead of the target as it is brought to the shoulder |

for a newcomer to point the gun at a moving target. It calls for greater precision than does the swing-through method, a precision that in the early stages of their careers few newcomers possess. For this reason many shooting schools favour the swing-through method. As with swing-through, point and swing generates a degree of automatic lead.

Sustained lead

This is the method used by most top Skeet shooters, although an increasing number of Sporting shooters use it for certain targets, while some use it for all targets. Basically, it involves pointing the gun ahead of the target from the very start of the swing. The gun is pointed neither at the target nor does it start from somewhere behind it. Essentially, the shooter observes the target he is expected to shoot, and then he decides just how much forward allowance it requires. If he decides that it needs, say, five feet, he will position his gun in such a way that when the target appears he can move the muzzles of his gun ahead of the target, never allowing the target to actually catch or pass the muzzles. During the mounting of the gun the 'sustained leader' will be adjusting the forward allowance his

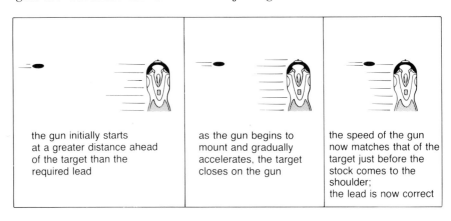

| the gun initially starts at a greater distance ahead of the target than the required lead | as the gun begins to mount and gradually accelerates, the target closes on the gun | the speed of the gun now matches that of the target just before the stock comes to the shoulder; the lead is now correct |

the gun pulls further away as the stock comes to the shoulder	with the lead correct, the shot is fired	the gun pulls away from the broken target in the follow through

muzzles are giving the target. By the time the gun has come to his shoulder, the lead is right and he pulls the trigger. A good follow through is essential with this method of shooting, and many top shooters will exaggerate this to ensure the gun doesn't stop as the shot is fired.

This method cannot be recommended for novices, since it requires considerable ability to read targets so that the correct lead can be decided upon. For this reason sustained lead can be classified as an advanced shooting method. Despite the fact that this sounds like a rather deliberate method of shooting it is still reliant on conditioned reflexes, and much of what occurs during the shot is unconscious. There is no automatic lead with this method.

Spot shooting

This is not a genuine method, rather it is a substitute for a method when all else will fail or be difficult to employ. Spot shooting is best described as corner cutting. It is very handy on the rare Sporting double, where its use on the first target allows an easy shot at the second. It is to be assumed from this that taking the first target using a more accepted method would

the gun comes firmly into the shoulder and the shot is fired	the gun follows through, leaving the broken target behind

The sustained lead series

47

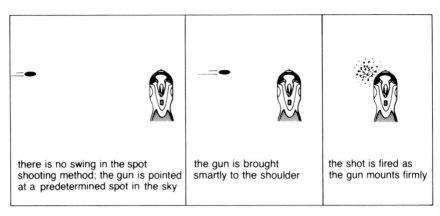

there is no swing in the spot shooting method; the gun is pointed at a predetermined spot in the sky	the gun is brought smartly to the shoulder	the shot is fired as the gun mounts firmly

Spot shooting – this is not recommended!

mean shooting it very late and thus jeopardising the chance of hitting the second.

Spot shooting is exactly as it sounds. The shooter decides precisely upon the spot in the sky where he intends breaking the target and then points the gun there and shoots the target without any perceptible swing. In order for this to work, the shooter must time the shot exactly to coincide with the target arriving in the right space in the sky so that the gun is pointing the correct amount ahead of the target as the gun is fired. As may be imagined, this method leaves a great deal to be desired since there are so many variables.

Anyone who has seen the *Starshot* television programmes will have seen the lower ring targets being broken after they have moved less than five yards. The shooter holds the gun just below the limit bar, calls the target and fires almost as soon as it appears. The method works, but only because these targets fly on exactly the same line, at exactly the same speed, and at very close range.

Although spot shooting should only be employed when there is no alternative, it can be highly effective in the right hands and with the right target. It has no place whatsoever at either Trap or Skeet events.

The Churchill 'no lead' method

Robert Churchill's shooting method relies on automatic overthrow. The idea is that if the shooter makes a fast enough swing, any required forward allowance will occur naturally. Churchill maintains that any lead should be entirely unconscious. The theory is based on the fact that there is a time lag between the intention to shoot and the actual pulling of the trigger. The Churchill method takes advantage of this fact, instructing the shooter to shoot 'at' the target and to allow the swing to give any necessary forward allowance.

This method seems to work for some people, and I must admit that anything that simplifies shooting will always get my vote. However, I have

48

yet to see a really top shot who can make this method work on all targets. Most people who use it find it works well on relatively close targets but soon discover that it is less effective as the range increases. For game shooters, many of whom fire less shots in a year than many clay shooters do in a week, a simple idea like this can work wonders. For serious clay shooting, however, awareness of lead seems to be essential.

Forward allowance

Telling a new shooter that he must point his gun in front of the target is all very fine. Quite reasonably he might ask: 'How far in front? What do I look at? Do I look at the gun? If I do, I notice that I cannot see the target properly. Do I look at the target? If I do, I cannot see the gun properly! Do I, perhaps, look at the space in front of the target? When I do that I have no idea where the gun is nor do I really know where the target is.'

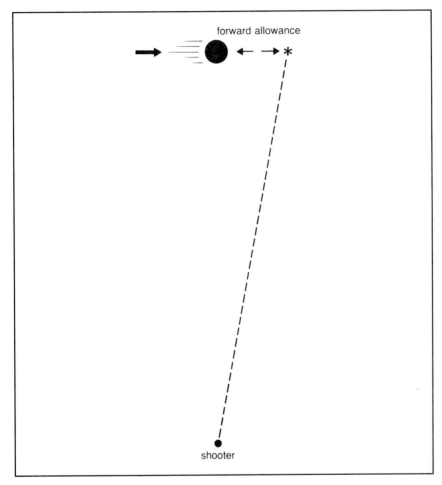

Forward allowance

The answer to his first question is that the amount of forward allowance depends on what the target is doing at the time. A close crossing target will generally require less forward allowance than a distant one. On the other hand, a close and very fast target might need as much or even more forward allowance than a distant but slow target! A distant and very fast target will need a disproportionately large amount of forward allowance, while a close and slow target will need hardly any.

By the time the poor newcomer has begun to absorb these pieces of information, and has found himself going cross-eyed trying simultaneously to look at gun, target and the space in front of it, he will be feeling very confused and frustrated.

It would be no less confusing if a coach were to try to teach tennis or squash, by attempting to explain the angle at which the racket met the ball for all the many shots encountered during a game, and then went on to explain that the player should look at ball, racket and the spot on the court where he hoped the ball would be heading. The whole business would be quite impossible and most players would give up in despair!

The same applies to shotgun shooting, and the sooner the newcomer absorbs the fact that shotgun shooting is quite unlike rifle shooting, the better for him it will be. The latter is a science, whereas shotgun shooting is an art. No good shotgun shooter thinks overmuch on a particular target, at least not while he is actually shooting it. All the thinking goes on beforehand. He has learned how a certain shot feels, by experience. He will observe the target, so that by the time he walks on to the stand to take his turn he knows exactly what he is going to do. He then lets conditioned reflexes take over, so that the unconscious is responsible for the success of the shot to a far greater degree than anything the shooter does at the conscious level.

There are many examples in clay shooting which illustrate that this is so. At ISU Skeet, for instance, two targets heading in exactly opposite directions take 1.6 seconds to travel from the trap houses to the out of bounds markers. These targets are released at random any time up to three seconds after the shooter has called 'Pull!' Yet at the top level both these targets will be broken almost unfailingly, usually within 1.4 seconds of the targets emerging. The novice will find the feat quite impossible, and many people, allowed to point with their finger instead of a gun, will find it very difficult to point at the two targets within the time allowed. It is only possible with a gun because the shooter, through constant practice, has absorbed the feel of the shots and is thus able to allow conditioned reflexes to do most of the shooting for him.

At the end of all this, does the newcomer know where to look and what to look at? Remember that shotgun shooting is an art, not a science. Treat it like a moving ball game and you won't go far wrong. Where to look? Not at the racket (the gun), not at the spot where you hope the ball will land (the space in front of the target), but at the ball (the target!) Your eyes must be focused sharply on the target. You will know where the gun is relative to the target because you are holding it, and cannot help but be aware of its position since it is right beneath your eyes. You will learn to 'read' targets so that you will know instinctively how much forward allowance they require.

The master movement

Relating the gun to the target is not something that happens once the gun has been mounted: it must happen *as* the gun is being mounted. This involves moving the gun to the target as the stock is coming to the shoulder. This very basic movement, done correctly, is the main difference between those who shoot good consistent scores and those who struggle to maintain a decent average. If you do this wrongly you can practise continually but you will never become a master shot!

This basic movement involves the following. Move the muzzles with or from slightly behind the target. As soon as you begin the shot, your head must not push down to meet the gun. As the muzzles are pointed towards the target, bring the stock smoothly up to your face. The muzzles must not be allowed to dip even slightly towards the ground during the gun mount, but must be kept pointing on the flight line of the target throughout the swing. As the gun comes into your face, nudge your shoulder forwards and upwards to meet it. It is not good technique to pull the gun back into the shoulder. By thrusting up and forwards, the shoulder provides a firm bed for the butt of the stock.

Essentially, the correct technique is a constantly moving gun mount. Bringing the gun to the face and shoulder *before* starting to move the gun to the target is a very common mistake, and is the main reason why so many people shoot below the standard of which they are capable.

Sporting

The history of Sporting

Sporting clay shooting is the direct link between clay shooting and live bird shooting. Sporting clay targets were first devised by the newly emerging shooting schools that appeared before the turn of the century. These were run by the well known gunmakers of the day who, through the schools, hoped to attract a larger clientele to their gunmaking businesses.

The targets thrown were intended to simulate the flight of game birds, although judging by the writings of the day the trap machines that threw the targets had only enough power to throw the targets about 40 yards. Not unreasonably, shooting school targets at that time were held to be unrealistic, and too easy. As traps and targets improved, so the value of these shooting schools grew. So, too, did the complexity of the targets they were able to present to the shooter.

From these beginnings the Sporting clay discipline evolved. Whereas in the early days game shooters condemned clay shooting for being too easy, today this is certainly not the case. Now few game shooters can make anything of the fast and highly diverse targets that are found at a typical Sporting shoot. What began life as a practice facility for game shooters has become a fine sport in its own right, and it is likely that the majority of those who shoot Sporting clays seldom or never shoot at anything live. The game has lost the down market image from which it suffered for many years. Clay shooters are far from being frustrated game shooters who simply cannot afford to shoot the 'real thing'.

Sporting is without doubt the most popular form of clay shooting in the UK, yet it has only a limited following abroad. This is partly historical, in that the early shooting schools were peculiar to the UK; and partly that Trap and eventually Skeet were popular abroad long before Sporting appeared on the international scene.

This situation may soon change, however. I remember visiting the USA in the early 1970s and finding very firm resistance to any sort of clay shooting that was not Skeet or Trap. At one gun club near Seattle, Washington, the club manager, with more foresight than sense, had fixed an ABT trap on a platform at the top of a tall tree. His intention was to provide his members with very testing tower targets. Sadly it had gone rusty from lack of use.

During the mid 1980s, the USA began to introduce Sporting shooting,

Utilising the contours: a high target from the top of the hill

and by the beginning of the 1990s the sport began to spread throughout the North American continent. With this great American interest it is almost certain that Sporting, at long last, will achieve proper international recognition.

There are two forms of Sporting: English and FITASC. The former is shot under the rules formulated by the English Clay Pigeon Shooting

53

Association (CPSA), which features a certain number of shooting stands. Each stand presents to the shooter a number of identical doubles. On a 100 target shoot this will usually mean ten such stands with five pairs of targets on each.

Because of the very high entries attracted to this type of competition, this format often means a great deal of hanging around at each stand,

A FITASC shoot in spectacular countryside

awaiting your turn to shoot. One way of speeding up the traffic, and an essential one if people are not going to drop out of the discipline from sheer boredom, is to have more stands with less targets per stand. A number of grounds already do this, and a 100 target shoot with 15 stands is a very different proposition. It's more fun, because there is a greater variety of targets, and more testing for the same reason, and quicker.

International Sporting is shot under the rules of the Fédération Internationale de Tir aux Armes Sportive de Chasse (FITASC). The FITASC version of the Sporting discipline is more complicated to organise and requires a far greater commitment of equipment and staff on the part of the organisers. A FITASC Sporting shoot is shot in squads on a number of 25 target layouts. A major shoot of 200 targets will utilise eight such layouts, all of which are different. There is no doubt that, properly set up, FITASC Sporting is one of the most challenging and exciting of the clay disciplines, its only drawback being that it is also one of the most expensive. Because of the time it takes to shoot FITASC Sporting, major events are invariably oversubscribed.

The discipline has undergone a change intended to increase the number of shooters who can take part in a given event. Whether or not this is a change for the better remains to be seen, but many of the original objections seem to have been answered to most people's satisfaction.

In recent years an increasing number of very smart shooting clubs have appeared, and it seems certain that before long country club style shooting grounds will spring up, where the central theme will be clay shooting rather than, say, golf. Predictably, these places will be the exclusive preserve of the relatively wealthy.

Fortunately for Sporting shooting, the mainstay of the discipline will always be the club that transports its equipment to a rented field or wood once a fortnight, sets up its shoot, then takes everything away again when the day is over.

Shooting English Sporting

The first thing to realise is that any target that is moving and is in range may be legitimately called a Sporting target. Any target from any type of Trap layout would qualify, as would any Skeet target. Added to these are targets that roll or bounce across the ground, targets that come from low, medium and very high towers, targets that jump straight up from the ground, targets that dawdle and those that go like an express train, targets that curl and twist in flight, targets that fly along well beneath the level of your feet, targets that come from behind you, targets that come towards you, targets that dive into the ground, plus just about any other target you can think of.

Just to add a further twist Sporting also features a variety of different target types, too. These are as follows: the 110mm Standard, as used in Skeet and Trap; the 110mm Rocket, a sort of solidly built shallow profile

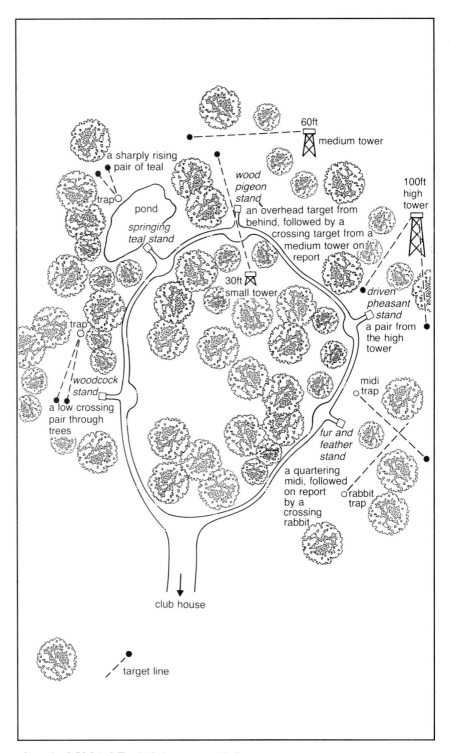

A typical 50 bird English layout, with 5 pairs on each stand

Top sporting shooter George Digweed in action at High Lodge
Shooting Ground

standard target that maintains its speed well and is difficult to break; the
self-explanatory 110mm Rabbit; the 90mm Midi, a very nippy smaller
version of the standard target; the 60mm Mini, a tiny target that slows to
a crawl within yards of leaving the trap; and the Battue, a sort of flat disc
that is unshootable (and almost invisible, too) when it's edgeways on and
yet which always rolls over to show its face just seconds before it dives
straight into the ground. Cunning shoot organisers will sometimes throw
targets from a tilted trap, or throw targets upside down, both schemes
calculated to make life just that little bit trickier.

An average shooter will hit his fair share of the targets presented, while
the top shooters will get well over 80% of them. As with any other
discipline, much of the difference between success and failure lies
between the ears. Among individuals of equal ability it will be the one
with the greatest determination and confidence who will win.

Shooting cages raise safety margins for English Sporting

Observation plays a big part in Sporting shooting

Observation

If carefully watching a Skeet or Trap range prior to shooting is beneficial, then it must be doubly so with Sporting, where frequently the targets thrown will be unique to that shoot. 'Reading the target', that is, noting the angles, speeds and directions of each target, is important. So too is discovering what type of target is being thrown. For instance, mistaking a midi for a standard would mean a wild miscalculation as to how the target should be handled. Make sure you know what you are shooting at.

There will always be an optimum place to take each target, very often this being decided by the behaviour of the other target of the double. As an example, take a right angle crossing target that is followed on report by one flying straight away. It makes sense to try to shoot the crosser so that the gun is perfectly positioned to point straight at the going away target. Taking the crosser earlier or later than this would make the second target unnecessarily difficult. The best shooters take great pains to establish exactly what they must do on each stand, and if they bother to do it so should you.

It will be seen from these comments that much of the secret of success is having a very good idea of exactly what is required before you walk on to any stand.

Ready position

For a number of years now English Sporting rules have allowed the shooter to call for his targets with the gun already in the shoulder. This is an unfortunate development, since it gets away from the idea of simulated 'real' shooting, where walking around with the gun already in the shoulder would be not only impractical but also very tiring. It is also poor shooting form, and is actually detrimental to your shooting. If you don't believe this statement, just go to a major shoot and see how many of the top performers do it. You will find that practically none of them does. If it was in any way an advantage to start gun mounted then they would all be doing it.

For the absolute beginner, gun up shooting will admittedly allow quick progress to a certain level, since it eliminates one of the more difficult aspects early in a shooting career: that of learning to mount the gun. But I firmly believe that the newcomer who perseveres with the gun down starting position will eventually be the better shooter.

Starting with the gun dismounted permits a quicker and smoother attack on the target. It also makes automatic the necessary slight dismounting of the gun between the first and second target of a double, which enables a rapid yet smooth transition from one target to the other. Finally, if you value your skill with a gun, learn to shoot gun down as it's better in the long run.

A good Sporting ready position is easy to adopt. Get the muzzles up and the stock tucked just under your armpit. This will encourage you to start

Top Sporting shot Barry Simpson in a classic ready position

your swing by pushing forward with your left hand, effectively pointing the gun to the target. This simple movement gets the gun quickly on to the target without any apparent effort, since the amount of swing required to catch the target is then minimal.

Contrast this with the shooter who allows his muzzles to point too high, or more likely, too low, and who holds the stock well down by his side. Either way he has to move the muzzles a long way in order to bring them to bear on the target and he has to raise the stock a long way to his shoulder. This takes a long time and creates lots of room for error.

60

Forward allowance

For many years theories about forward allowance have occupied shooters and shooting writers almost, in some cases, to the exclusion of all else. At one time certain writers claimed that forward allowance was unnecessary, and by suggesting this they caused great confusion. What they ought to have said was that conscious forward allowance was unnecessary for some people. A combination of reflexes, timing, and hand-and-eye co-ordination allow some people to shoot without being aware of making any forward allowance.

Unfortunately, this led many shooters to think that forward allowance was not necessary, conscious or otherwise, and this of course is nonsense. Some people can shoot without ever being aware that they have given their targets any forward allowance. But most of us have to allow the gun to swing ahead of the target, to a greater or lesser degree, or we will miss behind it. How far we shoot in front of a target depends on how we see it.

What is certain is that all targets, unless flying right at the gun or right away from it, will need forward allowance to some degree. How you personally see it, and this is all that matters to you, might be quite different to how your shooting partner sees it. But if you are both connecting then it doesn't matter.

What you have to do is go out and shoot to learn your own personal sight pictures. This does not mean that you have to learn how to aim your gun like a rifle. What it does mean is that you must learn the feel of the shot, and as you learn to shoot better, so your perception of forward allowance will change from something consciously directed to something that occurs automatically, without conscious guidance. But it needs plenty of practice on all types of target.

Sporting stands

Although the target possibilities at Sporting are almost without limit, it is possible to loosely categorise the different types of stands a shooter will encounter. Of course one 'Springing teal' stand may bear no resemblance to another with the same title, but shooters will know that the target or targets on these stands are going to start at ground level and rise very steeply. Let's look at how the various stands might be handled.

Driven

This is the nearest equivalent to the true 'game shooting' stand from which Sporting was derived. Driven targets fly basically towards the shooter, usually in pairs. The easier stand will feature 'driven grouse' or 'driven partridge', the names suggesting that here are two targets that will be coming in quite low and quick.

As with all Sporting shooting a good ready position is vital. Get the

A good solid stance from A.J. Smith

muzzles up pointing towards the place where the targets appear, and tuck the toe of the stock just under your armpit. From this position you can pick up your target quickly.

Although the targets might be released simultaneously it is unlikely that they will both be flying right over your head. Generally speaking, if one of them is straight over you and the other is heading left or right then take the straight target first. This is common sense, since this target will give you the least amount of time to shoot it. Taking it first will allow you to shoot it out in front of you, whereas if you take it second it will be very difficult, flying low over your head, or it will be already gone.

To make both shots as easy as possible, a good stance is essential. For this pair, stand to favour the place you intend to break the second target. Your weight will slightly favour your forward foot. Once you have set up properly you can now just turn to face the front, ready for the straight target.

Point the muzzles just behind it as it appears, bring the muzzles up to it as you are mounting the gun and catch it just after the gun beds into your shoulder. With your eyes holding it in perfect focus shoot as the gun swings through it. Notice that your weight should transfer more on to your front foot as you take the shot, but don't exaggerate it.

As soon as the first target is shot switch your attention to the second. At the same time ease the stock slightly from your shoulder. The purpose of this is so that you can make a whole new shot at the second. Place the muzzles on the line of the second target, and immediately start catching it as the gun is brought once more to the shoulder. Once again shoot as the gun swings through the target.

The time between the two shots is a lot less than it takes to read this sentence, and plenty of dry practice will make the transition from the first to the second position much smoother and snappier.

A tricky version of this type of stand is one where the targets are on you in a flash. I remember one particular stand at a major shoot where shooter after shooter was coming off, shaking his head having missed many targets. These targets popped out just above some bushes, usually a second or two after the shooter had called, and were over your head and gone almost before you could mount the gun. They weren't quite as quick as station eight Skeet targets, but near enough. And there were two of them!

One of the top shooters went on, shot the lot without any apparent trouble, then came off grinning. He had noticed that if you knew where to look you could just see the targets flick through the middle of the bushes, some ten yards before they appeared. He had spotted this and was moving to his first target, gun perfectly on line, well before it appeared above the bush. He shot this target just as it showed itself properly and, with his skill, the second was a formality – a perfect illustration of careful observation.

Springing teal

Springing teal can be very easy or very difficult, depending on how they have been set up. The simple ones, usually in simultaneous pairs, jump up from the ground some ten yards or more in front of the shooter and go straight up and away. Many shoots use rocket targets these days, as they climb quicker and further. Standard target or rocket, both show their vulnerable face to the shooter and so don't take much breaking.

Set up for these targets so that you are facing their line of flight. Decide which of the two targets you are going to shoot first and set the muzzles on this line. The first few yards of the target's flight is going to be very quick and something of a blur, so ignore it. Instead, hold the muzzles about a third of the way up the target flight line between the ground and the top of the target's trajectory. If you start with the muzzles lower than this you will be forced to swing fast to catch the target, but because it will be losing speed quickly you stand an excellent chance of overswinging it and missing over the top.

When you call for the targets, the one you have selected to shoot first

*Top all-rounder, US shooter Dan Carlisle shooting Sporting with a model
303 Beretta semi-automatic*

will zoom past your muzzles quite quickly. As soon as the targets leave the
trap get the gun moving upwards. As the target just passes the muzzles,
you smoothly catch it and re-pass it and shoot without hesitation.

You must then slightly dismount the gun, set the muzzles on the line of
the second target and repeat the swing. The difficulty here is that by the
time you catch the second target, it will have slowed almost to a crawl. It
may even have stalled completely and be about to fall from the sky. Shoot
right at it immediately. Forget about shooting just under it or just over it.
Get the target cleanly focused and don't hesitate.

It's worth remembering that Springing teal are always easier to shoot
on the way up than they are on the way down. Indeed, shooting them
rising might be insisted upon within the shoot rules. Also a target that is
falling is an accelerating target, and one that is at the mercy of any wind.
Trying to shoot a twisting, sliding and accelerating dropping target is not
easy. Shoot it going up or at least just as it stalls.

A more difficult type of Springing teal is one that flies edgeways on to the shooter. It is not only flying straight up but also slightly sideways, too. If it happens to be flying away as well then this makes it trickier still. 'Reading' the target is all important here, since you must have a clear idea in your mind as to what you intend to do with it. Carefully observe the flight line of the target, decide the best place to take it, then shoot it accordingly. The shooters who make a mess of this stand will be those who walk on unprepared and shoot 'scared'. Give it plenty of thought and shoot with confidence.

The quicksilver style of World and European FITASC Sporting champion Mickey Rouse

Quartering targets

In any Sporting shoot quartering targets of one sort or another will feature on many of the stands. A crossing target is one that is flying across you without actually coming much towards you or going much away from you. A quartering target is doing the opposite. It is flying mostly towards or away from you but also flying at a bit of an angle to you.

A crossing target requires a relatively big swing with the emphasis on

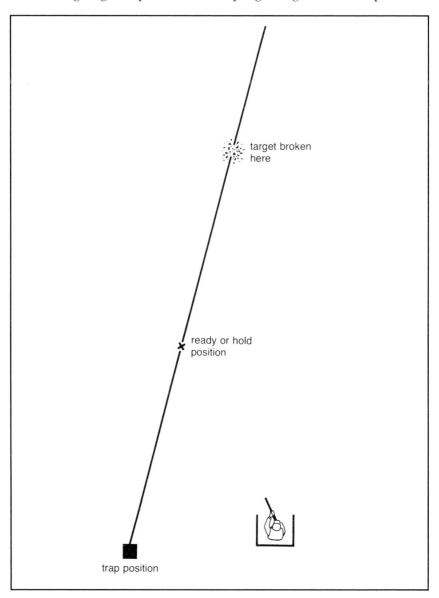

The quartering target viewed from above

follow-through and correct judgement of forward allowance. A quartering target places far less importance on these factors and far more on a good set-up and excellent timing.

The first thing to realise about a quartering target is that its speed is not particularly important. The rate of angle change, the deflection angle, is what determines the speed of your swing. A direct 25 yard crossing target flying at 40 mph will need far more swing and forward allowance than a quartering target that starts 10 yards to your side and flies away at a slight angle across you at 70 mph. It's rate of angle change that matters, not target speed.

Quartering away

Assume a target flying like the one described, which is shown in the illustration. Here the target starts to the left side of the shooter and flies at speed away and slightly across, landing directly in front of the shooting stand but 100 yards away. How should you shoot it?

The natural reaction is to point the gun as far back to the trap as possible. By doing this you imagine that you will give yourself more time. However, all you will do is guarantee that the target will zoom past your barrels and be heading well down field before you've even realised it's gone.

First of all you need to decide where you want to break the target. 40 yards out from the trap is too far, since this sort of range puts heavy demands on you and your shot pattern. 25 to 30 yards is more realistic. Having made this decision now stand so that you are facing this 'break area'. Remember, as always, to use a narrow stance with your leading foot pointing to where you hope to break the target. Your weight should just favour your leading foot.

The flight line of the target, or the bit of it that you are concerned with, is that section between the trap and your selected break area. With your gun in the ready position, set the muzzles over the break area and on the target flight line, then turn half of the way back along the flight line to the trap. You are now in a good 'ready' position.

Look back almost to the trap and call for your target. It will still zoom out, but this time you will be prepared for it. Having seen the target appear, slowly set your swing in motion so the target will catch and just pass the muzzles of your gun. Continue to accelerate your swing, bringing the gun smoothly to your shoulder as you do so, catching the target just after you've mounted the gun. With the gun still gradually accelerating, shoot without hesitation just as you pass the nose of the target. Throughout the swing your eyes must be riveted to the target, and must certainly not be allowed to look at the rib or the bead.

This minimal forward allowance surprises many average shooters, who automatically give a fast target a lot simply because of its speed. Remember that target speed is not as critical in deciding forward allowance as the angle at which the target is flying to the shooter.

British Sporting champion Gary Phillips uses a 32-inch barrel Miroku Trap gun for Sporting

Quartering pair

The quartering target just described could easily be one target of a pair, the other target being something altogether different, such as a rabbit or tower bird. On the other hand, there could be a pair of identical quartering targets, and if they are thrown simultaneously then they present a difficult proposition.

Where any simultaneous doubles are concerned it always makes sense to shoot the rearmost target first, so that you can just continue your swing to catch the second. If one is flying lower than the other, then take this one first. If you take the high target first, you will spend valuable time trying to find the second, since it will be hiding somewhere under your barrels.

This is an obvious common sense approach to target selection. It does go slightly wrong when you stand and watch the targets, since what starts as the leading or highest target will sometimes change after a few yards into the trailing or lower target. The point to note is the position occupied

Gary Phillips shows perfect gunmount and balance on an overhead target

Leading all-rounder Andy Harvison in the ready position for a high target from behind

by the targets at the point where you will be shooting them. If wind or poor trapping means the targets are all over the place, then you will have to abandon these suggestions and just shoot them as they come.

However you decide to handle them, remember to shoot each target as though it were the only target in the sky. Only when you've shot the first should you turn your attention to the second.

Targets quartering in are discussed under the section, 'Driven targets'.

Targets from behind

These tricky targets can be anything from fairly straightforward head skimmers to those that are thrown from the top of a high tower. They are set up in such a way that it is impossible to take them as incomers, either from the constrictions of the safety cage or because you are backed up tight to a tree or hedge. Whatever the reason, they are a going away target but a very different proposition to the target that gets up near your feet and flies away. Let's discuss lower ones first.

Anyone familiar with Skeet will handle the overhead low target from behind without any trouble at all. The way to tackle it is to look up and forward, not up and back. Look about midway between where the target appears and the place where you intend to shoot it.

The muzzles must be on the target's flight line and pointing at about 30° to 35° to the ground. The purpose of this hold position is to force yourself to move the gun down with the target, never up to meet it. When the target appears, just push the gun forwards as you begin to mount it, making sure that the target never passes the muzzles. You don't want it diving under the gun or you'll be in all sorts of trouble. As you mount the gun, just keep the muzzles slightly below the target. As the gun comes to your shoulder, shoot without hesitation. The sight picture as you fire will be of the target just sitting on the muzzle.

For those higher targets from behind, say 30 feet plus, the principle is the same, but with a few modifications to the hold position and also to where you look. The problem of forward allowance also comes to the fore here. First, you should look back more to the trap, although only right back on a very high target. On a medium high target the muzzles should be held correspondingly higher than on the head skimmer. How high you hold them is determined by your own swing and reaction time. You must be able to keep the muzzles ahead of the target all the time.

Before calling for these higher targets you will need to rehearse in your mind exactly what you intend to do. They are not the reflex shots that the low targets tend to be. You will have to visualise the target appearing and your gun moving off ahead and under it, and staying there as the gun comes smoothly to your shoulder. How far ahead and under is something you will have to work out for yourself. If you haven't practised these targets, then your first few attempts can be quite a surprise. You have to get used to the fact that the gun is being swung in a totally unfamiliar way

George Digweed concentrating on a target coming from behind him

— downwards — and that if you have not tried this out before finding it in a competition then you are going to struggle.

It's a classic example of sustained lead shooting. Decide on your forward allowance before you call for the target, then make sure the muzzles stay out ahead of the target as you smoothly mount the gun. Once the gun is in the shoulder and still moving downwards — ahead of the target — shoot. Trying to hold a long careful swing on this type of shot is fatal. The longer you hang on to it, the further away from you it's going to get.

Rabbits

The rabbit is one of the easiest targets there is. The reason is that it is much easier to read than an airborne target. Judging range is easy – the target is on the ground so is hardly travelling at any subtle angle — and it is not all that quick, either.

The problem most shooters have with rabbits is that they overlead the target, giving too much forward allowance. This is often caused by a misunderstanding of a succession of earlier missed shots by other shooters.

The trouble is caused by the shot impacting on the ground in the vicinity of the target. The shot is fired and misses ahead of the rabbit. It strikes the ground and kicks up great clouds of dirt and grass (if there's any grass left

Shooting on a downhill rabbit stand

at this point in the competition). The dirt kicks up, but only after the rabbit has whizzed on its way. The resulting spurt of jumping ground appears behind the rabbit, making it seem as though the shot has gone behind. It's surprising just how far you have to shoot ahead of a rabbit in order to make the ground kick up in front of it — several yards at least.

The best way to shoot rabbit targets is to use sustained lead, that is, to keep the gun moving ahead of the target all the time. First of all decide where you want to break the target. This is often decided for you by a limit post or a tree stump. Shoot the rabbit after this point and it's counted as a loss. Usually though, even on the toughest rabbit stand, you have plenty of time to shoot it.

Stand so that you are comfortably facing the 'break area', then turn back to where you will pick up the target. This will be determined by the need to stay ahead of the target all the time. Bring the gun only as far back as is consistent with you keeping the muzzles pointing in front of it. The muzzles should be on the line of the rabbit. Of all targets, the rabbit demands that your weight is very much on the forward foot and that you are leaning towards the target. If you try to stand upright, you will send your shot charge right over the rabbit. Crouch down and hunch up and you won't be able to swing properly.

How much lead you allow the target is determined by its range, although rabbits are rarely more than 30 yards away, and often much closer. Using sustained lead a close 15 to 20 yard target will need no more than a foot to

A simple rabbit trap cocked and ready

18 inches, a 25 yard rabbit about 2½ feet, and anything further about 3 feet or so. Rabbits certainly don't require the 6 to 8 feet so many people think necessary!

Call for your target and start moving the muzzles ahead of it as soon as it appears. Adjust your lead as you are mounting your gun and fire as the stock beds into your shoulder. Don't track the target – shoot without hesitation.

Now, what if it bounces? If the rabbit is taking a series of small hops then ignore them; keep your eyes firmly on the target and shoot it accordingly to plan. Any small deviations will be taken care of automatically. Bouncing rabbits present you with a slow airborne target that will definitely not deviate from its path. Just make sure you shoot it before it descends and you will hit it without any problems. The biggest mistake is to wait until it comes down and then to try to shoot it. It might just take another big bounce, and already you are running out of time. Don't waste time — get it shot.

Tower targets

Most towers come into the 'driven target' category handled earlier. The others – and there are not many of them throughout the world – are quite unique. These are the towers that throw truly high targets, those of 100 feet or more. Of these, the highest in the UK is found at the Roundwood Shooting Ground in Hampshire. It is nearly 150 feet, and few shooters ever properly come to terms with its targets. This is hardly surprising since even a dead straight target is on the very edge of shotgun range, and well outside the normal shooting experience. However, there is no reason why towers in the 100 to 120 feet bracket shouldn't be handled with competence. As always, knowing how to set about handling these targets is much of the battle.

There are two ways to take these very high birds. One way is to take them like any other straight incomer, only later. The other way some modern shooters adopt is to turn sideways on to the tower target and pretend it's a crosser. Let's look at the traditional way first.

The important point to remember about these high birds is that it is no use trying to take them early, out in front. If they are already on the limit of sensible range when they are directly over your head, then they are well out of range when they are out in front of you. You can break them there, but you'll waste an awful lot of ammunition trying to do it!

There is only one place to take them and that is right above your head. To do this requires that you are able to bend freely beyond this point. If you creak as you swing your gun to the vertical position, and then come to a dead stop, you will never hit high straight targets. Plenty of bending exercises are recommended for those whose backs aren't quite what they ought to be. You must be able to swing the gun well beyond the vertical.

There are three possible stances for this target:

(a) stand with your feet close together and with the weight on the forward foot, leg braced. The rear heel lifts off the ground as you arch your back

(b) stand with your feet close together and with the weight on the back foot, leg braced. The front heel lifts off the ground as you arch your back. These two are classic game shooting stances which work well provided you are fairly flexible, and are slim and lithe

Shooting instructor David Olive takes a straight-over tower target by turning sideways

76

(c) for the more solidly built, stand with your feet further apart, weight on the back foot, rear leg bent. The front heel lifts slightly, but much of the arching back to the target is achieved by the bending rear leg, and the back is less strained.

Which of the three you adopt is up to you, but go for the one that allows you maximum bend with minimum effort. You need to be able to swing the gun smoothly and freely right through this target without being distracted by twinges or a feeling of tightening up.

The place to point the gun is at or just slightly above the tower. If the stand is close to the tower – cutting down on the time available to shoot the target – then get ready by bending slightly backwards before you call for the target. Once the target is on its way get the gun moving, the muzzles slightly behind it and right on its flight line. Start the gun mount as you begin moving the gun, and accelerate your swing as the gun comes to your shoulder. Push the gun well through the target, bend well back to help keep the gun moving, and be sweeping away from the target as you pull the trigger. This sweeping away is an integral part of the high target shot, and it must be done very consciously if the shot is to succeed.

On these super-high targets some very fine shooters, and some leading shooting instructors, advocate giving the gun a 'flick' forward as the gun is fired. One of the best high pheasant shots of my acquaintance always does this, and he pulls down pheasants from great heights. If nothing else works then it's worth a try, although I would try using a normal accelerating swing before resorting to these tactics. They have a nasty habit of going wrong just when you need them most!

An interesting point with these targets is that when shooters miss they always attribute their failure to a miscalculation in the forward allowance. This may well be the problem, but having watched very many shooters struggling on this type of target it's a fact that nearly as many miss to the side as miss behind. Many shooters unconsciously drag the gun offline in their attempt to swing back and through the target. Most right handed shooters will send their misdirected efforts up the left hand side of the target, although not always. So when you are taking this target be as aware of line as you are of lead. Keep it straight.

The modern method of taking these high targets is to stand sideways to the tower and take the target as a crosser. To my mind this creates as many problems as it solves, although some shooters seem able to manage it. To me the only reason for turning like this would be because you lose sight of the target. It's not a way around bending backwards, because you have to bend even more acutely, and hold the position throughout the shot rather than just at the end. For shooters who shoot with an eye closed, it can often be the only way to take these high birds. Sorting out the forward allowance is part of the problem, but the main one is holding the muzzles on line. It's all too easy when shooting from this position to dip a shoulder and drag the gun way off line, usually under the target. This is one to dry practise frequently if you expect it to work for you in a competition.

Top Sporting shot John Bidwell with his 27½ inch barrel Browning

Suddenly deciding to do it when the bending back method has just missed you a couple of targets is asking to miss all the rest, too.

Crossers

Any target can be a crosser – a tower target, a rabbit, a long midi, even a springing teal. By definition a crosser is any target that flies across your front without also flying towards or away from you. It can be ten yards away, or 40.

Of all the targets in a Sporting competition, the wide crosser is likely to cause as much trouble as the high tower, although with less reason. Perhaps surprisingly, few small shooting grounds ever throw proper long crossing targets, so that many shooters view them with a degree of circumspection when they encounter them at a big shoot. This is not the place to discover that you are not too sure how to handle them. You must practise crossers and gain confidence in your ability to shoot them.

Before you worry about long range targets, sort out how to shoot the closer ones first. A Skeet range is as good a place as any to practise a close target, and if you get the chance to have a Skeet range to yourself for an hour or two then all the better. Check that it's all right with the shooting ground (you cannot do this if others are shooting Skeet with you). If the staff don't mind, start your practice by taking station four targets a pace or two in from the station. This will give you a nice close target of around 20 yards, but even this will demand a good swing and a proper follow-through.

The classic Skeet shooting method is sustained lead, and I believe that this is the best way to shoot any relatively close range target. I have my doubts about its effectiveness on longer shots, and by far the greater majority of Sporting shooters shoot these, and all their targets, using swing-through. Let's look at the close Skeet targets using this method.

Decide where you want to break your target, probably a bit past the centre peg, then stand so that your stance and gun is comfortably facing this break area. With your weight slightly favouring the forward foot, turn back to your hold position. This will be a few yards out from the house. When the target emerges it will just pass the muzzles and you must then start to accelerate the gun in order to catch it and re-pass it. Keep your eyes fixed on the target, smoothly mount the gun as you are catching it, pass it and shoot as soon as you have overtaken it. Make sure you follow through.

This might seem a complicated way to shoot a target that could more

Top Sporting shot A.J. Smith, a strong man who shoots a relatively light gun

easily be shot sustained lead, but it is practice for much longer targets. Take shots like this from both the low and the high house, then move back to the station. Repeat the same procedure, then move back two or three paces. It's surprising how much difference even this will make to how much extra forward allowance will be required. You cannot think about it in feet and inches, of course, but get the gun swinging through the target and learn the feel of the shot.

Once you can break targets like this you can stretch the range of the shot to 27 yards. Again, it will feel very different from the closer targets, requiring as it does a correspondingly greater forward allowance. Absorb the feel of swinging away from the target as you pull the trigger.

To take longer shots than this you will probably have to move away from the Skeet range and practise longer shots at a sporting ground or shooting school. The progressive way of practising, gradually increasing the range, is a good way to learn the right feel for crossers. If you move backwards and cannot connect, simply return to where you just were and re-establish the feel of those targets. Then move back again and concentrate on making a good swing through the target. Remember to shoot with the gun pulling away from the target.

Many shooters, when taking crossers, completely forget about elevation. A large number of long range crossing targets are missed underneath, and if you make what seems to be a perfect shot, yet it doesn't connect, then there is an excellent chance that this is where your shot has gone.

Keeping control of the muzzles is important on all shots, of course, but particularly on these long crossing targets. Mounting the gun too quickly can cause the muzzles to dip, as can setting up at address with the muzzles held too high. At address, when waiting for your target, make sure the muzzles are on the target flight line, never higher, and concentrate in practice on keeping the muzzles on line as you are mounting the gun. Plenty of dry practice can go a long way towards making this movement automatic.

Going away targets

Quartering away targets, springing teal and overhead targets from behind are all going away targets of a kind, but they are not true going away targets. A true going away target gets up at or near your feet and flies straight away from you. It ought to be very easy, and handled properly it is. Yet many shooters miss these targets, and this is almost entirely down to gun mount errors.

First of all you must stand properly. Set your stance to face the flight line of the target, and get your weight on your forward foot. The gun must be carefully positioned on the target flight line and the muzzles should be held on the same level as the target. Position the heel of the stock just under your armpit.

Mickey Rouse is one of those top shooters who uses a 32-inch barrelled gun

Don't look at the trap; look out to where the target is going to be flying. Call for the target, and as soon as it comes into your view fix your eyes to it and point the muzzles straight at it. The underarm stock position will encourage you to point the gun parallel to the target's flight line and will help prevent a 'target-missing' dip of the barrels. With the muzzles on the target, bring the gun smoothly to your shoulder and shoot the instant the gun beds into position. Done properly, the target will be hit every time.

81

Special targets

Midis

These little 90mm whizzers feature prominently in FITASC competitions and are frequently seen in English Sporting events, too. They fly quicker off a given trap than does a standard target and they maintain their speed well. They are no more difficult to shoot than a standard target, and they break well when hit. The trick is not to confuse these targets with standards. If you shoot a midi thinking it's standard, you will overlead it far too much. If in doubt, ask the referee.

Minis

These 60mm targets are so small that many shooters are frightened they could fly right through the pattern. This won't happen at anything other than very long range, and then only with open chokes. These fragile 'bumble bees' need only one pellet to break them.

They are not really very good targets. Having little mass, they slow down almost as soon as they leave the trap, and they hang in the sky just 'asking to be shot'. They look very easy and they are, providing you shoot them with determination and are not tempted to draw a bead on them. Swing the gun smoothly at them and shoot without hesitation.

Rockets

These are strange targets, being the same diameter as a standard target and yet of greater bulk. Despite their colourful name, they fly slower off the trap than does a standard target, and yet because of their mass they maintain speed better and are more durable. Wherever a rocket is the target, particularly if it is a long range one, use Trap ammunition with 7 shot and if you have multi-chokes then a tighter pattern won't go astray, either. It needs a solid hit to break it.

Battue

This target probably causes more frustration than all the others put together. It's a wafer thin target that flies fast and level for half its flight and then usually tilts on edge and dives into the ground. Unless absolutely forced to do so you should never try to break this target when it is presenting itself edgeways on. It will break quite easily if you hit it in this position, but because it is so thin it is hard to focus on and therefore difficult to judge properly.

Shot as a driven target it is not too difficult. It is showing its vulnerable face and, provided you don't shoot too slowly, this is quite an easy target. It becomes difficult when it is presented as a crosser. The time to shoot it,

A perfect setting for a Sporting ground: Doveridge Sporting Club

assuming it is rolling and dropping, is just as it rolls over and shows its face. This is just before it starts to dive, after which it gets really tricky!

Sustained lead is a fine way to handle the target. You can decide the lead you are going to give the target and then swing in such a way that the gun mounts to your shoulder just as the target rolls over. This is the moment to fire. A degree of low shooting should be built into your swing as insurance against the target dropping as you shoot. If you take it a second later than this, you will have to build in a lot of low shooting, because the battue will be heading towards the ground very rapidly.

Trap

Trap shooting disciplines of one sort or another are shot the world over. With the great variety available there is a Trap discipline to suit just about everyone. Regardless of how difficult or easy an individual Trap discipline may be, they all share the same basic characteristic. They all feature targets that fly away from the shooter.

How fast, how high and how angled the targets fly depends on the discipline, and there are some where two targets are released simultaneously rather than the usual single. These latter are games which have derived from other single target Trap disciplines, and few shooters view them as serious disciplines in their own right. For most, Trap is a single target game.

International Trap disciplines

There are several international Trap disciplines and all feature fast targets, some of which are very sharply angled. Olympic Trap (O/T) is the most testing, with five trap Universal Trench (U/T) running a close second. Automatic Ball Trap (ABT) is the third international Trap discipline and the most regularly shot. Its popularity is helped by the ease with which it can be set up with relatively little capital outlay.

A fourth international discipline, Double Trap, was tentatively introduced by the International Shooting Union (ISU) in 1988 as a third Olympic clay discipline along with ISU Skeet and Olympic Trap. It was intended that Double Trap would make its Olympic debut at the Barcelona Games in 1992, but owing to considerable apathy on the part of shooters towards Double Trap it may yet be sidelined or, at best, suffer the ignominy of being merely a 'demonstration sport'. A short explanation of how this game works will be given later in this chapter. It is possible that Double Trap could eventually die from lack of interest.

A further international Trap discipline, 'ZZ', is based on the shooting of a plastic disc held in the centre of a propeller. Five propellers are spun by machines until at the shooter's call one of the five is released. The target whizzes away, ducking and weaving, and is very tricky to hit with any consistency. Not being a clay discipline in the strict sense of the word, it is not proposed to examine this any closer.

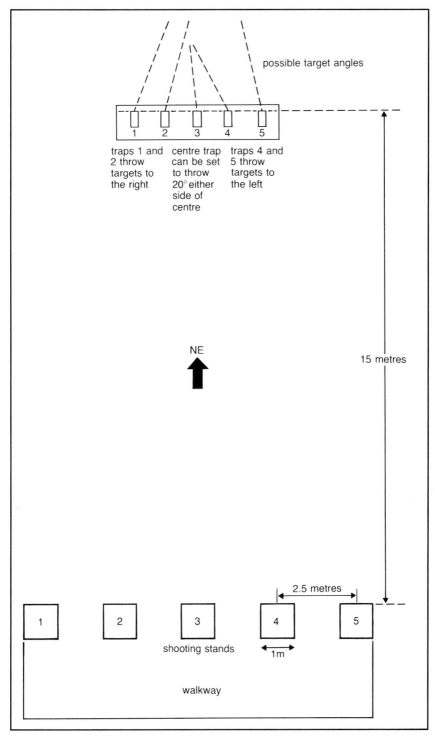

possible target angles

traps 1 and 2 throw targets to the right

centre trap can be set to throw 20° either side of centre

traps 4 and 5 throw targets to the left

NE

15 metres

2.5 metres

shooting stands

1m

walkway

Universal Trench layout (5-trap)

Down-The-Line

Down-The-Line (DTL), and its many derivatives, is the most straight-forward of the Trap disciplines. The targets are relatively slow, vary the least in angle and not at all in elevation. It is the easiest of the Trap disciplines, and a newcomer can soon be breaking quite high scores in a comparatively short time. Two shots are permitted at each target, with a first barrel kill scoring three points and a second barrel kill scoring two. This handicap places a greater demand on accuracy than would otherwise be the case, and the winner will be the shooter who breaks the most targets with the least number of shots. Winning at this discipline is not about mastering difficult targets, but is about hitting every one of them, preferably using just one shot per target.

There are several factors that you must take into account if you are to make the best of your ability at DTL. An important one is stance, and this is related to the target angles encountered on the various stations. Look how the targets are distributed on each of the five pegs.

Peg one: target angles vary from dead straight to an extreme left hander. No right hand targets at all.

Peg two: angles vary from a shallow right hander to a quite wide left hander.

Peg three: equal angles left or right.

Peg four: angles vary from a shallow lef   ler to a quite wide right hander.

Peg five: angles vary from dead straight to an extreme right hander. No left hand targets at all.

It is easy enough to break your fair share of targets just by standing in an ordinary stance facing the trap, but most leading DTL shooters stand to favour the most difficult target that they can encounter on a given station, this being the most widely angled target. They will stand facing left of centre on pegs one and two, to handle the wide left hand target; dead centre on peg three where either angle is possible; and right of centre on four and five.

The actual stance is with your feet no more than about eight inches apart at the heel and with the weight evenly distributed. Your left foot should be forward, and assuming the position you are facing is twelve o'clock your left foot should face one o'clock and your right, three o'clock. As the gun is mounted into the ready position, so the weight is pushed slightly more on to the front foot. This must not be carried to excess, because overcommitting your weight forward will make it difficult to move freely. Your posture ideally wants to be more or less upright, with your legs slightly bent to help flexibility of movement.

It is possible to stand more open or squarer than recommended. Neither of these extreme positions works well at the faster international disciplines, so it is likely that those who use them for DTL shoot well despite their position rather than because of it.

The address position

Peg one

Here the hardest target will be a wide one to the left, so it makes sense to stand to favour it. Your twelve o'clock positon won't be the centre of the trap house, therefore, but a point several yards to the left of it. Face this point then turn back to the house.

Peg two

The harder target will still be a left hander, so your twelve o'clock position should still favour it, but less so than on peg one.

Former England DTL champion Grayham Webb showing a high and left hold position on peg 2

87

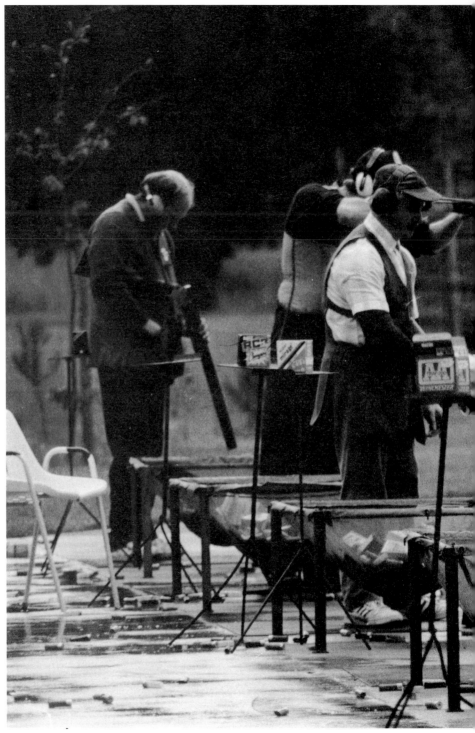

A picture of concentration. Leading Trap shooter Ian Peel (nearest

camera) awaits his turn to shoot

Peg three
Your twelve o'clock position here is dead centre of the trap house, since you can get targets flying equally wide in either direction.
Peg four
Twelve o'clock on this peg is a yard or two to the right of the trap house.
Peg five
The widest of the right hand targets can appear here, so twelve o'clock is several yards outside to the right edge of the trap house.

Where to point the gun at address

Like a good stance, adopting a sound gun point position is yet another way of making DTL as easy as possible. There are several schools of thought as to where the gun should be pointed on each peg. One says that the gun should always be pointed at the dead centre of the trap house, and level with the roof, regardless of the peg on which the shooter is standing. By doing this the shooter is always properly aligned for any straight target yet is handicapped on the wide crossing targets, which he must chase a long way to catch. Other shooters advocate a hold position that favours the widest crossing target. This works as follows.

Peg one: gun point is the top left corner of the trap house.
Peg two: gun point is midway between the top left corner and dead centre.
Peg three: gun point is dead centre.

An exaggerated address position, holding well below the mark, from Italy's Agostini

90

Peg four: gun point is midway between dead centre and top right corner.
Peg five: gun point is the top right corner.

The objection to this method of moving the gun point across the trap house is that, other than on peg three, the gun is always misaligned for the straight target. It only requires a slight correction of the muzzles to bring the gun on-line, however, and the shooters who favour this method prefer to suffer this slight handicap in order to gain a start on the wide crossing targets.

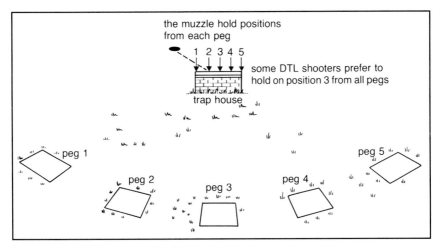

Hold positions for Down-The-Line

Gun hold height

Many shooters point their guns at the top of the trap house while others take a higher hold above the house. The purpose of this is to cut down the movement to the target, which is always rising, and thus enable the shot to be taken quicker. The disadvantage of this is that from an elevation point of view the muzzles are off track right up until the moment they settle on the target. For this reason some shooters distrust this method, but it's worth trying if you have trouble taking your targets quickly enough. It is also a good way to shoot targets that are climbing into a headwind.

Gun mount

Since the Trap shooter calls for his target with his gun mounted, it's easy to imagine that the act of mounting the gun is less important in Trap than it is in, for example, Sporting or Skeet. In fact, mounting the gun in Trap is as much an integral part of the shot as it is in any other discipline, and it must be done smoothly, efficiently, and correctly.

All shotgun shooting relies on good rhythm and timing. For Trap this rhythm begins the moment you close your gun and prepare to mount. A good pre-mount position is with the stock just tucked under the armpit,

Top DTL shooter Andrew Womble in action

muzzles slightly up and pointing just over the gun point position. You should fix your eyes on this position then mount the gun on it. Exactly how to mount the gun is described in the chapter on training. Once it is mounted you then let your eyes look out, taking in as large an area as possible beyond the trap house. It's important that nothing is held in focus at this point, not the trap house and definitely not the rib or bead.

If your preparation is good and your mind is steady, then most of the hard work is done. Now call for the target. Your eyes, focusing on nothing, will latch on to it immediately. Smoothly swing the gun after the target and pass it, shooting when instinct tells you to. This will be as the muzzles pass the target if it's a crosser, or as they settle on the target if it's a straight one. The pulling of the trigger is not directed by conscious thought, and if you try to check alignment of gun and target before you shoot then you will lose that instinctiveness so vital to good shooting in any discipline, and you will miss.

Squads

Most regular DTL shooters like to shoot with a squad of their own choosing, people with whom they are familiar and who shoot at their pace. This is fine while it lasts, but what happens if for some reason you must shoot with a different squad, or you find yourself in a shoot-off?

It's very easy, if shooting with a very fast squad, to be swept along by them to the detriment of your own shooting. The same applies in a shoot-off, where suddenly finding yourself alongside an unfamiliar shooter can throw your shooting out of joint. It might be worthwhile to get used to shooting with different people occasionally.

Other DTL games

Single barrel

This is DTL with only one shot permitted instead of two. It's a very popular discipline in the USA.

Handicap

The handicap referred to is the increased distance the shooter stands from the trap, the yardage back depending on the skill of the shooter. In the UK the maximum is 23 yards, but in the USA 27 yards is where the top shooters must perform, and with one ounce of lead and one barrel. This is very compulsive both to shoot and to watch.

Double rise

Yet another DTL derivative, this time with two targets being released simultaneously. It is a good deal more testing than DTL, not only because of the two targets instead of one but also because wider angles are possible. Like the other sub-DTL disciplines, though, Double rise is very much a poor relation and is comparatively rarely shot.

Above and right: DTL squads in action

Automatic Ball Trap

Much of what has been said about DTL applies to Automatic Ball Trap (ABT), and indeed where stance and set-up is concerned there is little difference between any of the Trap disciplines. Like DTL, ABT employs just one trap machine, but usually it is a very different one. For a start ABT targets are a great deal faster than those of DTL, but there are other significant differences, too. The maximum possible angles to the left and right are much wider and there is variable elevation, too.

The lowest ABT targets would be partly obscured by a standard DTL box type trap house, so the ABT trap is positioned in a pit generally with a ground level steel roof. The nature of the trap machine means that the left angled targets emerge from the left of the trap house and vice versa. The stations are further apart than those of DTL, which means on pegs one and five it is possible to encounter very widely angled targets indeed.

For this reason most ABT shooters employ an 'across the trap house' method of gun point, similar to that of DTL shooters. On peg one the gun point is on the left edge of the trap house; it is midway between this point and centre on peg two; it is on centre at peg three; it is midway between centre and the right edge on peg four and on the right edge on peg five.

The height the muzzles are held is also determined by the fact that the targets emerge anywhere along the width of the trap house. If they are held high, then there is every chance that a target could slip out without the shooter seeing it until it's too late. Most ABT shooters point the gun at address at the front lip of the house. Many hold even lower than this, believing that they will see the target better.

Top Trap shooter Kevin Borley shooting ABT in Scotland

Great Britain team shooter Ian Coley at ABT Skeet

Stance and foot position should also favour the widest angled targets likely to appear on each peg. For instance, on peg five the maximum angled target to the left is only slightly left of straight, whereas the maximum angled target to the right flies almost at 90° to the shooter. It makes sense, then, to stand to favour this wide right angled target.

ABT is an excellent discipline in its own right, yet it is not sufficiently fair in its target distribution to have earned true international acceptance.

Kevin Gill in action at the British Olympic Trap Grand Prix

Because of the nature of the machine that throws the targets it is possible that one shooter could receive all easy angled targets while another could get a succession of difficult angles. In practice it seldom works out like this, and during a 100 target competition the target distribution tends to average out quite well.

The view of most Trap shooters is that ABT is an ideal stepping stone between DTL and the true international disciplines, Universal Trench (which most shooters refer to as 'Five Trap') and Olympic Trap.

Olympic Trap

From ABT to Olympic Trap (OT) is a big jump, not just in the quality of the competition but also in the degree of acceptance on an international level. Olympic Trap is the ultimate Trap discipline, in degree of difficulty, costs for the shooter, and for the outlay required to actually install an OT layout.

The fifteen traps used ensure a tremendous variety of target angles, speeds and heights. Speeds vary from fast to faster, and with the wide angles and heights, the OT shooter has to be fully awake for each target.

Although there are wide angled targets in both directions they don't appear on any particular station as they do on, for example, DTL and ABT. The stance and foot position should be one that enables you to turn freely

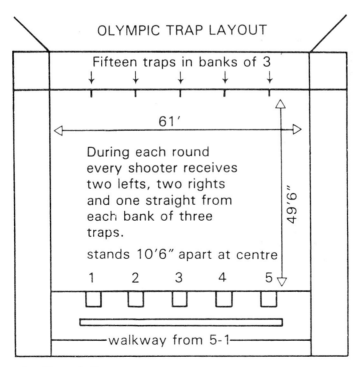

Layout for Olympic Trap

in each direction on all stations, therefore. Assuming straight ahead to be twelve o'clock, then the left foot should point to one o'clock and the right to three o'clock. This position in fact favours targets going to the right, which is always the hardest direction in which to turn if you are a right handed shooter. The distance between the feet should be as narrow as feels reasonably stable, which for most people means keeping the feet about 8 inches apart at the heels.

Marco Venturini of Italy, one of the world's top Olympic Trap shooters

Gun mount

In any discipline the gun mount relates the gun to the eyes and, done properly, provides a stable position from which the gun may be fired without leaping about in the shooter's hands. For OT the gun mount is no different to that of any other discipline, although to watch the time some people take to prepare themselves, wrapping themselves around the gun and burying their heads on the stock, you would think there was a vast difference.

Essentially, the purpose of the gun mount is to relate correctly the gun to the eyes, and then having mounted the gun to move the whole unit, shooter and gun, into the hold or address position. Many shooters combine these two movements, mounting the gun directly on to their chosen hold position. Others mount the gun well above their hold position and then bend slightly forward until the gun is pointing at the chosen spot. Some mount the gun well below their hold position and then bring the gun up to it.

Leading Olympic Trap shooter Kevin Gill prepares to take a target

Of the three possibilities the first, mounting directly into the hold position, is the least complicated and allows the shooter to call for his target without further preamble.

Consistency in gun mount is just as important here as it is in any other discipline, and since you need to be able to focus your full attention on the target it is not something you should be worrying about while you are shooting. Practise gun mounting regularly and make sure you do it properly.

Taking the shot

Where should the gun be pointed once it is mounted? This is a subject for experiment, and it is likely that your hold position will change with the weather conditions as well as with the various OT layouts that you shoot on. The ideal hold position will be one that affords you as quick a view of the target as possible in the prevailing conditions, and this will also be affected by background and target colour. Possible hold positions can be anything from several feet above the mark to a point actually below the

British team shooter David Lloyd shooting Olympic Trap

Italy's Carlo Dana is one of Olympic Trap's most stylish shooters

mark. It is something to experiment with, since the ideal position may have to be varied according to the conditions you are shooting in.

With the gun mounted, the next step is to call for the target. But where to look? As with DTL and ABT, look out beyond the lip of the trench and hold a soft focus on nothing in particular. Allow your eyes to see as much of the area out ahead of the trench as possible but without letting them hold focus. Then, when the target appears, your eyes will immediately see it and focus on it.

It's tempting with such a quick target to start the swing when the target's exact direction and trajectory are only vaguely perceived. This is when the target is still a blur. Starting to swing at this point is asking for the gun to be off-line when you eventually focus the target cleanly, and you don't want to have to make corrections if you can avoid it. So, wait that fraction of time it takes to see the target clearly and then shoot it.

The actual shot is very much a matter of instinct, and for this reason OT is not a good discipline at which to start a shooting career, since you won't

Winston 'Wink' Halcomb of the USA shooting Olympic Trap using a Krieghoff with an adjustable stock

have any shooting instincts! Much of the success of the shot lies in the preparation leading up to it – concentration on the job in hand, a good gun mount, knowing where to look and knowing where to point the gun prior to calling for the target.

The acoustic release system mandatory for proper OT shooting guarantees that the target is on its way almost before you have finished calling 'Pull!' The gun is swung along the target flight line, gradually accelerating until it overtakes the target. This is when the shot is fired. There must be no conscious decision to pull the trigger, it just happens as a result of conditioned reflex action.

The second barrel

One good feature of all the international Trap disciplines is that you get two shots at each target, and breaking the target with either one counts as one point. Without the second barrel, international disciplines would be, with few exceptions, very low scoring affairs. There are the odd 25 straights shot at OT, but these are heavily outweighed by the number of 25s shot with half a dozen or more second barrels.

If the first shot is a matter of instinct, then the second barrel is exactly the same — only more so. The elapsed time between a first barrel that misses and a second that kills is barely a few milliseconds, certainly no time for conscious thought. So, the second barrel is again the product of instinct. If the first shot missed, presumably either the elevation was wrong, the direction was wrong, or the timing was wrong. Possibly it was a combination of all three. There is no time for analysis. Your eyes should still be fixed on the target. Keep watching it, get the gun swinging again and shoot it.

Non-shooting people watching the Trap disciplines often wonder what it is the shooters are firing at when they have already broken the target. They are shooting the pieces, the purpose being to keep the second barrel working smoothly. This is important, especially for a shooter who is steadily breaking his targets with the first barrel. Shooting the bits ensures that when a target eventually evades the first barrel, as one surely will, the shooter will be tuned up ready with a quick second.

Universal Trap

The targets of this discipline are slightly slower than those of Olympic Trap, yet since all five traps are shot from each station the maximum angles are more acute. The most acute angles are experienced on stations one and five, and foot positions and stance should reflect this. On stations two and four the same rule applies, though less so, with only centre station three allowing a stance to handle equally targets that can go widely in either direction.

The gun hold positions on each station can be similar to those of ABT, that is, pointing the gun to the right of centre on stations four and five, and to the left of centre on stations one and two. As with all international Trap disciplines, it is very important to hold a wide view of the area beyond the trap pit so that the target can be picked up quickly.

Double Trap

Double Trap was introduced in 1987 especially for the Olympic Games. Having been around for a very short time it has already been adapted because the original game was basically unfair, and seemed to appeal to few shooters of any discipline.

The original Double Trap featured one fixed line trap positioned alongside an ABT trap, with basic shooting stands from a typical Olympic Trap layout. Each shooter would shoot five doubles from each stand, changing stand after each double, making each round 50 targets per shooter. The object of this was to push more shooters through a competition in a short time.

Shooters take part in a particular discipline because it interests and challenges them. The original Double Trap did neither of these and died from lack of interest.

In the revised version there are three traps, arranged in the same fashion as one bank of Olympic Trap machines but with the outer traps facing out rather than in. On each stand a shooter gets two doubles from the centre and left traps, two doubles from the centre and right traps, and one double from the left and right trap, again making 50 targets per round. This is certainly a fairer way of doing things but still it has not led to a great following for the new discipline.

This is probably because the original thinking behind this discipline is flawed. When clay Trap shooting began it did so as a substitute for live pigeon shooting. It caught on because people wanted to do it. Had they not wished to it would not be around today. Sporting clay shooting evolved from the desire of early gunmakers to take advantage of the new clay targets. They used them to offer instruction to their game shooting clients, and shooting schools began to appear. It was an obvious progression to develop these natural targets into a competitive form, and Sporting was born. Even Skeet, the least natural of the clay shooting sports, was never forced upon the clay shooting population. Some American friends invented it as a means of improving their field shootings, others tried it, liked it, and the new game gradually evolved into modern day Skeet.

With Double Trap the situation is entirely different. The ISU has decided that shooting needs speeding up, and they reason that with Double Trap they have found the answer. Unfortunately you cannot make shooters take part in a discipline in which they have no interest, and this still seems to be the situation with Double Trap.

Those who do shoot Double Trap are shooters whose main interest is elsewhere, and who shoot it as a diversion from their usual discipline. I don't believe that there are as yet shooters who specialise in it to the exclusion of all else.

To be fair to the ISU, the invention of Double Trap was a direct result of the requirements of television, and more specifically American television. Air time during the Olympic Games is extremely expensive, and from an advertiser's point of view it is important that any Olympic sport must be sufficiently 'watchable' to guarantee a good audience.

Shooting, unfortunately, is hardly compulsive viewing to those who don't participate. Double Trap was created for two reasons. Firstly, the targets are easily kept within camera view at all times and, secondly, the event is begun and finished on the same day rather than in three days, as with Trap and Skeet. It's a great shame that we should have a discipline forced on us by the requirements of a mass television audience. But the shooters will decide if the discipline is to stay, and we will have to wait and see what the outcome is.

Skeet

Skeet was created purely as a clay shooting game by a few American shooters in the 1920s, to provide themselves with light relief from the rigours of the game shooting field. The game they invented was shot on 12 shooting stands encircling a single trap, and was eventually modified so that there were two traps, placed 42 yards apart at either end of a semi-circle. The shooting was conducted on this semi-circle. From this unlikely beginning Skeet developed and became the game as we know it today, with a high house and a low house (originally a tree stump and a taller tree stump).

Back in those early days it can hardly have seemed likely that this game was to become one of the two Olympic clay disciplines, yet it appeared for the first time in the Olympics at the Mexico Games in 1968.

The game shot in the Olympics, under the auspices of the International Shooting Union (ISU), is the most difficult of the several Skeet disciplines. The easiest, and arguably the most popular, is that shot under National Skeet Shooting Association (NSSA) rules in the USA, where many thousands of people shoot the discipline every weekend across the whole North American continent, Canada included. It also has a fair following in the UK, too, where many US military bases allow UK residents to use their Skeet facilities.

The UK has its own version, known as English Skeet, a derivation of NSSA Skeet.

Since all three Skeet disciplines (ISU, NSSA & English) use the same layout, and mostly the same stations, there are many similarities of stance and procedure. Because of this, all three disciplines have been included here, with the various differences noted station by station. The three are not so different, and in fact NSSA and English are in many ways identical. Before we begin, here are the fundamental differences between the three.

NSSA Skeet

The rules of this game have remained unchanged for many years. Reference to the Skeet diagram will explain where the stations are situated and also indicate the fixed flight line of the two targets. Basically, the rules give the shooter singles and simultaneous doubles on stations one, two, six and seven and just singles everywhere else including station eight. This makes 24 targets in all. The 25th target, assuming all others have been hit, is a repeat of station 8 low bird. If a miss occurs anywhere during the round, the shooter is required to re-shoot this target, bringing his total to 25. The targets must fly 55 yards in normal events and 60 yards in the bigger championships. This extra five yards, creating a faster target, make all the difference. Gun position is optional, many shooters choosing to shoot with the gun already mounted, and the target must be released the instant the shooter calls for it.

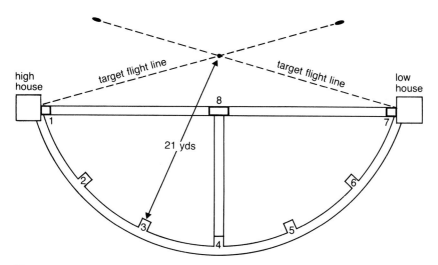

Skeet layout diagram

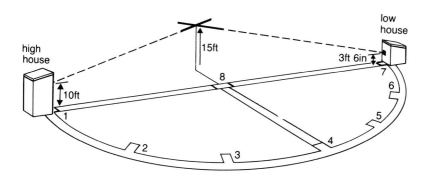

3-dimensional Skeet layout

English Skeet

The rules are the same as NSSA with the following differences. Singles and doubles are shot on stations one, two, four, six and seven with singles only being shot on stations three and five. Station eight is not used. On station four the shooter must nominate which target he will shoot first in the double. On station seven, assuming he hasn't missed, he can decide which of the two singles he will shoot as his 25th target. As with NSSA he must re-shoot the first target he misses during the round. Target distance is 55 yards, regardless of the event, and gun position is optional. With both NSSA and English Skeet 100 straight is a relatively common achievement, with most of the major championships being decided often after a prolonged shoot-off. In the USA it has been known for two competitors to shoot over 1,000 shoot-off targets before a decision is reached!

Ready to start a round of English Skeet

ISU Skeet

The international Skeet discipline is very similar to the original Skeet game as shot in the USA in the 1930s, although the targets are much faster. The target sequence is as follows. Station one: a single high house target then a double. Stations two, three, five and six: singles and doubles. Station four: singles only; station seven: a double; and station eight: two singles. This makes 25 targets with no optional or repeat single should a target be missed.

The targets must be thrown a minimum of 65 metres and a maximum of 67 metres. The target can be released any time up to three seconds after the shooter calls, and the stock must touch the hip bone and stay there until the target emerges. The random delay, the gun position and the extra speed of the target all conspire to make ISU Skeet rather more difficult than the other two disciplines. A 25 straight is sufficiently notable to warrant a round of applause from spectators and other competitors alike, and 100 straight is rare enough to be worth a celebration even at the highest level. At this level a winning score at this game will be anything around 195 ex 200 or better, with 200 ex 200 being very rare. For the majority of shooters, anything over 180 ex 200 can be considered pretty good.

Skeet shooting technique

There are two accepted methods for shooting Skeet, the swing-through and the sustained lead. I believe sustained lead to be the only worthwhile method for Skeet, and that using swing-through is just making hard work for yourself. I also have to admit to a certain bias, brought on by personal experience. When I began shooting Skeet it was as a result of watching NSSA Skeet shooters in action in Seattle, USA. They all used sustained lead, and I followed their example. Back in the UK I was attracted to the more testing ISU Skeet and saw no reason to change my way of shooting. At that time in the UK, in the mid 1970s, nearly everyone shot ISU Skeet using swing-through. I changed, and for several months shot very average scores indeed. For me the method worked all right in practice, but just fell apart in competition. I shot one 200 target selection shoot using swing-through, shot 165 ex 200, and determined never to use swing-through again. The following month, having returned to using sustained lead, I shot a 191 ex 200 and broke into scores of over 195 about three months later. From then on, swing-through for me has had the thumbs down as far as ISU Skeet is concerned! There are very good ISU Skeet shooters who use swing-through, as well as a number of good NSSA/English shooters who use this method, too. I am quite certain that they are making very hard work of Skeet shooting, though.

However, there are certain targets, when shooting ISU Skeet, that are

111

inevitably shot using the swing-through method. This is because sustained lead is simply not possible on the second targets on certain doubles. This will be expanded upon later.

The ISU Skeet ready position demonstrated by Lubos Adamec, a leading Czechoslovakian shooter

Preparation

A mixture of anticipation and nervousness is the right frame of mind to be in prior to any type of competitive shooting. The effects of this are explained elsewhere in this book. What is certain is that you don't want to be a nervous wreck, though many shooters get themselves into this state, and usually it's all their own fault. They lose their glasses, can't find their earmuffs, get the zip stuck on their shooting jacket, and all this with just two minutes to go until their round begins. This is not the way to prepare.

One of the more important preparations for a round of Skeet is to get to the field while the preceding squad is at about station four or five, and be completely ready. This means actually beginning preparations for your round fifteen minutes earlier than this, particularly if your equipment is several hundred yards from the shooting field.

Once you arrive at the field you can watch the targets of the squad already shooting. Are they on the right track? If not, how far off-line are they? Are they flying the distance? Are they being tossed about in the wind, or is either of them being consistently pushed down or up by a steady breeze? All these things can be observed before you walk on to the line, and this extra little bit of knowledge will give you a slight advantage over those who don't bother. Every little helps.

As soon as the preceding squad has finished many shooters like to warm up on various shooting stations, swinging their gun at a few imaginary targets. At English Skeet a couple of practice shots are permitted before the first round of the day, although they are not obligatory. Some shooters like to let the gun off in this way, and they often pick their least favourite

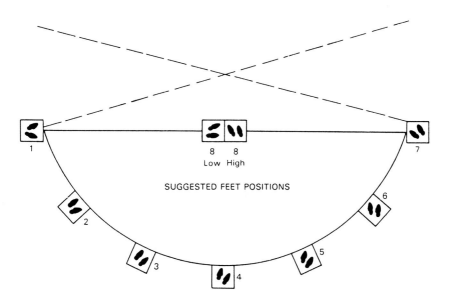

Skeet range diagram showing feet positions (the stations are 3' × 3')

target. Quite what it does to their mental well-being should they miss is another matter!

Practice shots are not allowed at ISU Skeet, although it is permitted to fire two shots on station one to clear the gun prior to each round. Some shooters like to do this, and if it appeals to you as a way of loosening up then go ahead and do it. From my own point of view, while never feeling recoil in any way during shooting, I always find that letting off the gun in this fashion rattles my teeth and thumps my shoulder. It also seems a dreadful waste of cartridges.

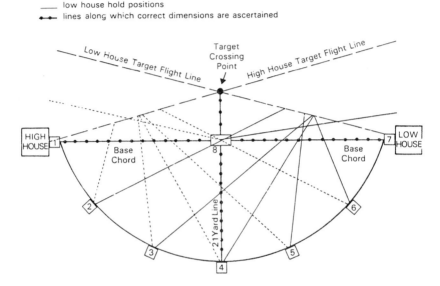

KEY ...... high house hold positions
_____ low house hold positions
•—•—• lines along which correct dimensions are ascertained

Skeet range muzzle 'hold' positions

Skeet, station by station

Stance

One of the many important factors that must be right if you are to shoot well is stance. Your feet are your only connection with the ground. If they are too far apart you will be unable to move freely, and if they are too close together you will be poorly balanced.

Your feet should be no more than eight inches or so apart at the heels, about the width you would adopt if you were standing having a chat with someone. A good rule for Skeet is to point your leading foot towards the place where you will be shooting the second target on any station where there is a double to shoot. The other foot should be a few degrees open from the leading foot. This stance is one I have always shot from myself, and one I would advocate to others. The golden rule is to always stand for the second target, both in the singles and the subsequent double. You

Classic ISU Skeet stance from Dunkel of Germany

The USA crouching style taken to its limits by Al Mullins in Montecatini, Italy

could stand in the position ideal for each individual target but this would be unwise since you cannot juggle your feet in the middle of a double, and singles ought to be regarded as rehearsals for the coming double. If you shoot the double by standing to favour the first target your swing will be severely compromised for the second targets on stations such as three (ISU), four (English/NSSA) and five (ISU). The first targets of a double require a relatively short swing, whereas the second target requires a relatively long one.

Balance
Skeet seems to cause a few people to get into the strangest positions, and it doesn't help that some of the regular winners falls into this category. The way to regard their success is as being in spite of their odd contortions, not because of them! The best way to stand is upright in a narrow stance, with weight evenly distributed between the feet, or perhaps just favouring the leading foot. There should be no forward leaning, or, worse still, leaning backwards. Over-committing weight in this way makes it very difficult to swing smoothly, and doubly difficult when the swing has to change direction.

The swing
In Skeet, as in any discipline, turning to the left or right means turning from the hips, and not simply twisting the shoulders. A good turn of the hips allows a full and free swing, whereas twisting the shoulders against the hips causes the swing to bind up. Twisting also disrupts the gun mount, and causes elevation problems. (See Training.)

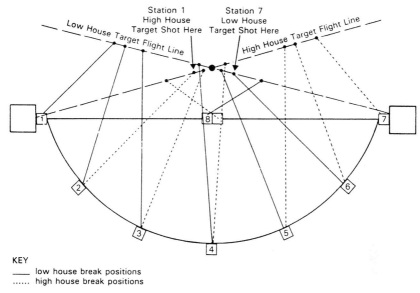

Skeet range diagram showing where the target should be broken from each station

Station one, high house single

ISU

This and station eight are the only ones where a practice gun mount is permitted. Some shooters always have a quick practice; others never do. I see it as a rehearsal for what is to come. Mount it once or twice, set the stock on your hip, then set the muzzles up with the barrels at about 40° to the ground. Make sure the muzzles are on the target flight line, then let your focus go out beyond the muzzles. Call for the target and don't move until you see it. If you get into the habit of moving as you hear the trap you can easily find yourself moving to the sound of adjoining traps, particularly when there are back to back Skeet fields.

When the target appears it will seem to be going downhill, even though it is actually rising. The correct move is to point the muzzles gently towards the target as the stock is brought smoothly into the mounted position. The relatively high ready position of the muzzles will guarantee a dipping motion of the gun, so there is no need to make any effort to shoot low. At no time should the target be allowed to drop beneath the muzzles. If it does, then you cannot see it, and your chances of hitting it are rather slim! Ideally, the target will be sitting slightly above the muzzles as the gun comes to the shoulder, and the shot must be fired immediately.

This is essentially a smooth shot, and must never be rushed. Even when mounting the gun at a relatively slow pace the target will easily be broken several yards before the centre. It is worthwhile watching the best performers shooting this target. Although it is broken very early, the actual movement of the gun is steady and controlled.

117

Mickey Rouse calls for his target in station 1, English Skeet

NSSA Skeet/English Skeet

Gun position is optional for both disciplines on all stations, and many shooters choose to start with the gun fully mounted. The advantage of doing this is that gun mounting errors are eliminated. The disadvantage is that it restricts movement and makes for a less fluid swing.

When shooting with the gun fully mounted, set the muzzles to point between ten and twelve yards out from the house on the target flight line. Look out over the muzzles, call for the target, then move the muzzles downwards as it appears, so that they are pointing just a fraction beneath it. Once the gun is moving smoothly, the shot can be fired. Never try to shoot this target with a completely stationary gun, hoping the target will run into the shot. This is very inconsistent and will mean lots of misses.

For those who prefer to start with the gun dismounted, the stock should be just out of the shoulder and dropped perhaps three or four inches, *never* right down in the ISU position. Remember, this position is deliberately included in the ISU rules to make ISU shooting difficult. Very few ISU Skeet shooters, given the option, would ever start with the gun down on their hip!

The most usual way is to mount the gun, then just drop the stock without moving the muzzles at all. The muzzles should be high enough that they intersect the target flight line some 10 to 12 yards out from the house. You then just look out over the muzzles and call for the target. The instant you call, the target will be on its way. With this relatively slow target there is never any need to rush, and indeed if you try to be too quick you can miss it. Let it come out, smoothly mount the gun, keeping the muzzles just below the target, and shoot as the gun comes to your shoulder. Since the gun has hardly any distance to travel before it is in position, this target will be shot early. Never try to shoot it too fast!

Low house single

This target is not shot as a single in ISU Skeet. In English/NSSA it is, and is considered to be one of the easiest targets on the field. It must not be treated too lightly, since championships have been lost when this target has flown on untouched!

With the stock mounted or slightly dismounted, the muzzles should be pointed well out of the low house, over the centre peg. This is to avoid the temptation to shoot the target too quickly, which is a fine way to miss it. Get the muzzles on or just below the target flight line, then call. Let the target come almost to the gun before starting the swing. Move the muzzles along in front of the target, maintaining a lead of no more than a foot, shooting the target when it is about midway between the centre peg and the high house. Some people let their low house bird come much further in than this, but it's asking for trouble, particularly if a wind is bouncing the target around.

Double ISU/English/NSSA

There is no such thing as a double, just two singles flying together! Doubles

119

are simply two singles shot in quick succession. On station one, the set up is the same as when shooting the high house single, since this will be the first target to shoot. The secret when shooting any double is to concentrate on one target at a time to the complete exclusion of the other. So shoot your high house target as though it were a single. As soon as you have seen it break then you can switch your attention to the second.

If you have shot your first target in good time, the low house target will just be coming to the centre peg. Simply reverse your swing, adjust the lead to about a foot and shoot the target coming in, not as it passes the house.

Station two, high house single

ISU
For many shooters this is one of the most feared targets on the field, and I must admit for the first year or so of my ISU Skeet career it caused me much anxiety. But, as with all things, there is a proper way to handle it and once you understand what's required this target can be brought under control. I think it is fair to say that it always requires 100% concentration, and although I shot many hundreds of rounds of Skeet without missing it I never took it for granted.

Stance and hold
Take a narrow stance and point the muzzles slightly right of parallel with the high house. Keep the muzzles, as you see them, slightly below the target flight line.

Many shooters try endless experiments with gun hold positions, stance and balance, and yet never come to terms with this target. I did the same thing for a while but about every other round, one and sometimes two, would get away. What finally made all the difference was discovering the correct place to look for the target. I used to look right back to the shute, but eventually discovered this was wrong for several reasons. For a start the target will emerge as a blur, and you will take time to adjust your focus. Once you have the target clearly focused it will be quite some way down the field. By looking back you also have to turn your head away from the gun and thus out of position. As your eyes are trying to adjust, focus so your head has to turn into the right position. All this while you are trying to mount the gun on a target speeding away down-field. Much the best idea is not to look back for the target at all. Look midway between the muzzles and the house, with your eyes holding an expanded and soft focus that takes in the whole area between gun and house without actually focusing on anything. This soft focus also helps you to avoid becoming jittery should the target take the full three seconds to emerge.

When the target leaves the shute, your eyes will pick up its movement immediately since the target will appear in your peripheral vision. This is the moment to begin your swing. The purpose of this immediate reaction is to keep the muzzles moving ahead of the target. As the swing begins, so your eyes will at the same time locate and focus on the target very quickly. Seeing the target, this quickly allows you to take a relatively easy swing at it, keeping the muzzles about a foot or so ahead of it as the gun is brought smoothly to the shoulder. As the gun beds into position, without hesitating or slowing the swing, the shot is fired immediately.

If the shot is taken correctly, the target will be broken some two yards before centre. It is possible to shoot it quicker than this, but you will snatch the gun mount and possibly miscue and miss the target.

One of the great ISU Skeet shooters from the USSR, Tamas Imnaischvili

Martin Elworthy, British Skeet champion in 1987, '88 and '89 · takes the high house target on station 2

English/NSSA

Although '2 high' is slower in these disciplines than in ISU, it is still afforded considerable respect even at the highest level. With the gun mounted or dismounted, the barrels should be held about parallel with the high house, although some shooters will bring the barrels slightly closer than this. The muzzles are held just on or slightly below the flight line. Because the target is released instantly, your eyes can look further back than when shooting ISU, but never into the shute. If you look at the shute, it will take time to readjust your focus to the target. So, look just out of the shute, holding a soft focus.

As soon as you have called, the target will appear, so begin to swing as you call. In this way the muzzles will remain ahead of the target. Adjust the lead to about a foot or perhaps slightly less and, with the gun smoothly swinging, shoot without hesitation. Those who start with the gun dismounted can time the shot to coincide with the gun mount. As with ISU it is a mistake to track this target or to start checking that everything is all right. Done properly the target will be broken two to three yards before centre. Although it is possible to shoot much quicker than this, *don't*!

Low house

ISU

This target is very rarely missed by experienced shooters, but it can be and therefore must be treated with the same respect as any of the more difficult targets. Stance and balance are the same as for the high house target, since they must also be shot as a double. Muzzle hold position is over station eight and just below the target flight line. Look for the target just out of the shute, and look carefully if it's a black target coming out of a dark background such as trees in shadow.

When the target appears, begin moving the gun immediately, although not quickly. The idea is to let the target come to the gun, but not to a stationary one. Begin mounting as the gun is moving ahead of the target. Adjust the lead to 2 to 2½ feet, complete the mount, swing the gun smoothly for a few yards, then fire and follow-through. The target will be broken halfway between the high house and the centre peg. There is no reason to miss this one, but when a shooter does it is often because he has allowed himself to relax mentally, having successfully shot '2 high'. Regardless of difficulty, all targets count one on the scorecard, so give this low target full attention.

English/NSSA

The technique is exactly the same as for ISU, as are the stance and hold positions. This target won't fly as steadily as the ISU version, being slower, and if you let it come in too far, particularly when it has a tail wind, it will be dropping quite a lot once it has flown a few yards past centre. The answer is to shoot it before it drops beneath the gun. With a strong tail

123

Taking the low house incomer on station 2, English Skeet

wind this can mean shooting it almost as soon as it passes centre. Even in the calmest conditions, get the target shot while it is still coming in, not when it is level with you or, worse still, when it has almost reached the limit marker.

Double

ISU/English/NSSA
If you can shoot the singles, then you can shoot the double. Set up for the first target, the high, in exactly the same way as you did for the single. Shoot the target in the same fashion as you did the single, without speeding up or jumping at the target. If you shoot it smoothly before centre, there is plenty of time for the second target. Make sure you see the first break before looking for the second; then reverse the swing, adjust the lead on the incomer and shoot it without hesitation.

In certain circumstances, perhaps after having shot the first target a little later than intended, the second will have to be shot swing-through.

Puldon of Cuba showing his unique finish to a double!

This is necessary when, having shot the high target, you find that the low is already to the left of the muzzles. The principle is the same, except that the target must now be caught and overtaken. Swing through the target and, as soon as a lead of about two feet is obtained, fire and follow through. This method is likely to be called upon when shooting ISU Skeet, but should not be required on this station when shooting the other slower disciplines.

Station three, high house

ISU

Station three is the first of the stations where both low and high house targets are true crossers. The high house target fairly 'zips' across the field and it is here that shooting sustained lead really begins to pay off. This target suddenly became more tricky in 1977, not because it was speeded up but because the ISU decided that doubles as well as singles would be shot on this station. Prior to this rule change, the high target could be shot in a fairly relaxed way. Following the new rule it became necessary to break it before, or certainly no later than, the centre. Shooting this target after it has passed centre makes the second one very difficult.

Stance and balance are the same as for station two, with the weight distributed to favour the leading foot slightly. The muzzles are held just below the target flight line and about midway between the house and the centre peg. This is where to point the gun when you are learning how to shoot ISU Skeet, but as you become more skilled the muzzles can be brought nearer to the house. It's worth experimenting with all hold positions, but particularly with this one. The closer you can hold the gun to the house, the better, always assuming you can react smoothly and quickly enough to keep the muzzles ahead of the target. The sooner you can start leading the target, the quicker you will break it.

As with station two high house, it is not a good idea to look right into the shute. Hold a soft focus just out of the shute so that your eyes snap on to the target the instant it appears. Make sure you are ready before you call for it, because if you are not, this target will be well down the field before you even start to react.

As the target emerges begin to move the muzzles ahead of it. At the same time begin mounting the gun. Initially, the muzzles will be pointing well ahead of the target which will quickly close the gap. The object is to get the gun moving at the same pace as the target so that it doesn't overtake the muzzles. Adjust the lead to about four feet and, as the gun mounts firmly into position, fire immediately and follow through. This adjusting of the lead may sound very difficult, but in practice it takes little effort and is soon learned. The great secret is to fire the gun without first checking that everything is all right. Make your swing and trust it.

The idea is to break this target a yard or so before the centre peg, and once it is mastered it is really one of the most satisfying of shots. So many

You're never too young to start! Richard Brickell, aged 14, with his British Junior ISU Skeet Championship cup and gold medal

potentially good Skeet shooters spoil the shot by checking to make sure, instead of shooting without hesitation. I have often thought, when watching someone struggling with this and similar targets, how easy it would be to improve their scores simply by tying a piece of string to the trigger of their gun and letting a good Skeet shooter control the timing of the shot!

127

English/NSSA
Although there is no double on this station for either discipline, the target should still be shot with a degree of urgency, and should not be allowed to drift on beyond the centre. The muzzle hold position need be only five or six yards out from the high house, the eyes looking just out from the shute. Smoothness is more important than speed; when the target is on its way, start the swing, adjust the lead to 3½ to 4 feet, fire and follow through. There is never any reason to break this one past centre, and ideally you will break it several yards before.

Low house

ISU
Theoretically this is easier than '3 high', yet I have seen a number of championships lost on this very target. Although an incomer, it is nevertheless a wide crossing target, actually presenting one of the longest shots on the Skeet field.

English Skeet lends itself well to shooting from a wheel chair

Stance and balance must be exactly the same as for the high target, since there is a double to be shot. Muzzles are held, as usual, just below the flight line and are pointed midway between the centre peg and the low house.

Look for the target just left of the shute, and pay particular attention if the background is at all similar to the colour of the target. I well remember watching a top shooter, who was leading a major competition, fail even to fire at this target. He was wearing dark glasses against the sun, and the black low house targets were coming out of a very dark background of tall conifers. He called for his target and was still waiting for it when the referee announced 'lost'. It had come out and had flown by without him ever seeing it.

When the target appears, start the muzzles moving immediately, remembering that the idea is to lead this one all the way. Adjust the lead to about four feet as you bring the gun smoothly to the shoulder. Without being too deliberate a fraction of time is allowed between the mount and the shot to check that everything is right. The shot must then be fired, breaking the target about five yards past centre. Don't track it steadily down the field beyond this point, because it will become increasingly difficult once it is more than ten yards past centre. If the target has a strong wind behind it, shoot it over the centre peg.

English/NSSA
The same rules apply as for ISU, but as the target begins to drop soon after it passes centre, it is good policy to shoot it over the peg or soon after. The hold position is about midway between low house and centre.

Double

ISU
This double is not as difficult as it appears, although when it was first introduced in 1977 it caused endless problems. Many shooters imagined that quick snap shooting was required, but in fact the rhythm of this double is exactly the same as any other: that is, quick, smooth but unhurried.

The set-up is the same as when shooting the high single, which will be the first target of this double. The first is shot in the same fashion as the single, but the second has to be shot using the swing-through method.

Having shot your first target, reverse your swing, being careful not to stop the gun dead just as you fire. The second target will be seen just to the left of the muzzles and you must accelerate the gun through it to a lead of some four feet, when you must fire immediately and follow through. A mistake a lot of sustained lead shooters make when shooting swing-through is to swing ahead of their target and then try to maintain the lead. To do this entails slowing the gun, and it will cause the shot to go behind the target. It's not enough to swing through the target: swing through and be swinging *away* from it as you pull the trigger.

Station four, high house

ISU

This is the halfway stage. You don't shoot a double on this station in ISU Skeet and because of this many shooters make the mistake of taking a long careful swing at both station 4 targets, regarding them as incoming targets. However, the best ISU Skeet shooters always treat these targets as outgoers, which means they shoot them over the centre peg and no later. It's by far the best way.

Stance and balance are the same as for the previous stations: weight very slightly favouring the leading foot and a narrow foot position. Since there is no double on this station, you can stand to favour the target, but don't overdo it.

Point the muzzles at the midpoint between the high house and the centre peg, and keep them just below the flight line of the target. As with station three, you can come closer to the house than this but there is not the same urgency to get the target broken early here.

Look just outside of the shute, eyes held in soft focus. Because it is flying almost at a right angle to the shooter this target cuts across the Skeet field very quickly, so be fully alert when calling for it. As soon as the target emerges start to swing, keeping the muzzles up on its line and ahead of it. Adjust the lead to four feet as you are mounting the gun and fire as the stock beds firmly into the shoulder. Follow through after the shot has been fired.

English/NSSA

Although slower than its ISU equivalent, this target still moves quickly across the field. The gun point position need be no further than a third of the way out from the house, between the house and the centre. From this position it should be quite easy to shoot this target using the sustained lead method. As with all targets that need to be shot sharply, the time to start the swing is the moment the target appears, immediately after you have called.

Get the gun moving so that the muzzles are leading the target by about 3½ to 4 feet and once you are swinging smoothly, fire. It is possible to track this target well past the centre, and break it. The longer you leave it, the greater the chance you will miss. As soon as you are swinging smoothly and you see the lead is right, shoot without hesitation.

Low house

ISU

This is the first of the fast low house targets encountered on the Skeet field that must be shot with a degree of urgency. The foot position and stance can be that of the previous target, although most shooters like to readjust themselves into a slightly different position, usually facing more to the left of the centre peg. There is no double to worry about, so changing your foot position doesn't matter as long as you don't overdo it. The muzzles are held, as usual, just below the flight line, and are pointed a touch closer to the low house than midway between house and centre peg.

Start moving as soon as you see the target, adjust the lead to around 4 feet and shoot as the gun firmly mounts. A very common error on all targets moving left is pulling the gun across the body instead of turning properly. Where the shot goes when swinging like this is pure speculation, but it is unlikely to be on the target.

Stay alert on this target, and doubly so if the background is at all awkward. If this one gets the drop on you, then you will probably miss it. Normally you should look for it just to the left of the shute, although where you actually look might need to be adjusted if the background is awkward. I remember one shoot in eastern Europe where to look anywhere near the house was a waste of time. Yellow targets emerged from a background of yellow bushes and were more or less invisible. Most of us ended up looking several yards out of the house, to the position where the targets first broke the skyline. This severely reduced the available time for shooting the target, but it was possible. Many were missed by those who failed to make the adjustment.

English/NSSA

This target should be shot in much the same way as the one from the high house. Point the gun about seven yards out of the low house, and keep the muzzles just below the flight line. Start your swing as soon as the target appears, adjust the lead to 3½ to 4 feet and shoot with the gun swinging smoothly.

Because this target can be shot very quickly, as can all English and NSSA Skeet targets, don't fall into the trap of shooting them faster and faster. Just before the centre is quite fast enough, and by shooting there you will be shooting under full control. On the other hand, don't be tempted to 'ride it out'!

Double

English only

In all Skeet doubles the rule is that the shooter must take the target from the nearest house first. From station four the houses are equidistant and the shooter has the option to shoot either first. The best solution is to take second the target that is flying best. The definition of 'flying best' is the target that, having past the centre peg, is flying level or perhaps is still rising.

Usually the wind will be the decider on how the targets are flying.

Whichever has the wind behind it will be dropping quite abruptly, and so this is the one to take first.

Having decided on your first target, stand to favour the second of your double. You can do this quite safely because you are going to take that first target quickly, before the swing begins to bind up.

Stand as though shooting the single, with the intention of shooting the target a yard or two before the centre. Avoid shooting quickly at the first target. This might seem to be what's required but there is more time than you think. Shoot it smoothly, then immediately reverse your swing and look for the second.

If you have shot the first target quickly, you will find that your muzzles are ahead of the second and that you can lead it in the same way as when it was a single. It is more likely, though, that you will have to catch up with the target and shoot it 'swing-through' style. If this is the case, then make certain that you do swing through. Don't just get ahead of the target and then try to shoot it sustained lead. Not only will this make for a late shot, but it will almost certainly mean a slowing gun and a shot that misses behind. So swing through, see the lead, and be swinging away from the target as you pull the trigger.

Station five, high house

ISU

This is one of the most difficult of the so-called incomers. It is one of the widest targets on the field and, for right handed shooters, it presents the more awkward left to right swing. Added to these factors is the target's speed.

To shoot it, stand facing the point where you intend to break it, which is about midway between the centre and the low house. Point the muzzles midway between the centre peg and the high house and just below the flight line. Look for the target just outside of the shute. It's important to begin moving as soon as the target appears, keeping the muzzles ahead of it. It appears to be coming in quite gently, but in fact it comes down the field very quickly.

Adjust the lead to about four feet as the gun is coming to the shoulder, bed the gun firmly into position, shoot and follow through. Lead on this needs to be about four feet, but I have frequently broken this target with six feet of lead and sometimes more. It takes a lot to miss it in front.

Particular care must be taken when the target has a strong wind behind it. It will dive very low soon after it passes the centre peg, so in these conditions it's best to shoot the target as it comes to the centre rather than later.

English/NSSA

There is no need to take this target much beyond the centre since, unlike

132

ISU, there is no double to shoot here. Stand facing just to the right of the centre peg, then turn to point the gun about ten yards out of the house, muzzles just below the flight line. Move as the target appears, adjust the lead to about four feet, swing smoothly and as soon as the lead is right fire and follow through. Although this target is not very fast it is easy to miss behind it. Keep the swing moving as you shoot.

Low house

ISU
This is probably the most missed ISU target, especially since it has become part of a double. It is out and gone very quickly, so you must be completely ready before you call. It's no good shooting the high target then casually turning and calling for the low one without giving it any thought.

Stand in the same stance as for the high house target, facing midway between the low house and the centre peg. The muzzles should be pointed a bit closer to the house than midway, so that you are forced to take the target early. Don't point them so close to the house that you cannot keep the muzzles moving ahead of it, though. As with all targets keep the muzzles just below the target flight line.

Visibility can be tricky on this target, because it is often emerging against a poor or mixed background. Because of this keep a soft focus just outside the shute, and be careful not to allow your eyes to focus on the background. If you stand and watch this target it will pass the muzzles in a flash and be gone down the field. So make sure you are ready to move the instant you call.

Move the muzzles smoothly ahead of the target and begin to mount the gun at the same time. The object is to adjust the lead to about 3½ feet and to get the gun firmly mounted two or three yards before the target reaches the centre peg. Fire now without any hesitation, and follow through.

This is a target that will benefit from plenty of practice. Because a double has to be shot here, it is important to get into the habit of taking the first target quite early.

English/NSSA
Despite being a bit slower than the ISU equivalent, this target gets missed more frequently than just about any other single. More shooters miss this one than they do 'high 2'!

Stand facing the centre peg, then turn back so that the muzzles are pointing about ten yards out of the low house, muzzles just below the flight line.

The target comes as soon as you call, so get the muzzles moving smoothly in front of it, adjust the lead to around 3½ feet, shoot and follow through. There is no need to hurry the shot, but don't let the target get past the centre peg before you shoot it.

133

Double

ISU

This is arguably the hardest double on the ISU Skeet field. The secret of success lies in the way you take the first target, the low one. Many people struggle to hit the second and think that the fault is with their technique on this target. This is possible, but more frequently the fault can be traced back to the way they take the first target.

Set your stance and muzzles as though taking the low house target, and make sure you are absolutely ready before calling. Shoot this target as though it were the single, that is, just before the centre peg. Reverse the swing the instant the target is broken. There is no chance of shooting the second target with sustained lead, unless it has been held up in a strong wind, so it must be shot swing-through.

This return swing must be aggressive otherwise you won't catch the high target, especially if it has the wind behind it. Catch it and push well through it, see a lead of at least four feet and fire, pulling more ahead of the target as you do. Any slowing of the swing, or hesitation, will mean a sure miss behind.

Station six, high house

ISU

At this stage, assuming you haven't missed any targets, it's easy to think you have finished the hard work and that a '25 straight' is a certainty. The round is far from over, however; there are still eight targets left to shoot, several of which are difficult.

The incomer on station six may be one of the easier targets on the Skeet field but, like all of them, it can be missed. Point the muzzles over station eight and keep them just below the flight line.

This target usually emerges against the sky, so visibility is no problem. As the target appears, get the muzzle moving ahead of it, steadily bring the gun to the shoulder and have it firmly mounted as the target crosses the centre point. Steady the swing, have a quick check that the lead is right, about 2 to 2½ feet, then fire and follow through. Done properly, this target will be broken halfway between the centre peg and the low house, although a tail wind may dictate that you shoot it earlier.

English/NSSA

Gun ready position apart, take this target in exactly the same way as recommended for ISU. In a strong tail wind it may be necessary to shoot it as early as the centre peg to avoid taking it when it has dipped abruptly and possibly dived under the barrels. Don't ride it right down the field.

Low house

ISU

Even though this is the low house equivalent of 'high 2', it causes less trouble, although any target can become troublesome if you don't give it full attention. Stand in a narrow stance and point the muzzles just left of parallel to the low house and slightly below the flight line.

Where you look for the target depends very much on the background. What you should *not* do is look right back to the shute. If possible look just out of the shute, eyes in soft focus. Some leading shooters look midway between house and muzzles, while others hold a soft focus right out by the muzzles. Experiment to find what suits you best.

Try only to react when you see the target, not when you hear the trap. You might, after all, be reacting to another trap entirely, and if you do this you will find it hard to recover. If you get into the habit of reacting to sound you will also find yourself reacting to the sound of shots being fired, and with three other ranges in use you will be jumping and twitching until the target appears!

As soon as you see the target start moving and mounting, adjust the lead to no more than a foot, mount the gun firmly and fire immediately. Ideally, you will break this target a few yards before the centre peg, but definitely no later than the peg.

English/NSSA

For this target you can point the gun parallel to the low house. Begin to swing smoothly the moment you've called for it. It only needs a small amount of lead, no more than a foot, and you can break it about four yards before the centre. Don't be tempted into riding this target. Get it shot as soon as everything is right, but never hurry. Skilled shooters can break this almost as soon as it leaves the house, but they never do. They know that rhythm and timing are far more important than pure speed, and that very fast shooting will upset both.

Double

ISU

As with all doubles the trick is to shoot the first target, in this case the low house, quickly and smoothly. Having shot it, reverse the swing. If you have shot it in good time, you can shoot the incomer sustained lead, in which case just repeat what you did with the single. Should you have to swing through it, then make sure you *do* swing through.

English/NSSA

Unless you really waste your time on the outgoer you can certainly shoot the incomer with sustained lead. There is plenty of time, but don't delay too long. Get it shot!

135

Station seven, high house

English/NSSA
This is the easiest target on the field, but many shooters have come to grief here. It is not caused by target difficulty, just by lack of attention or perhaps by trying to shoot too quickly.

Point the gun over the centre peg and don't move until the target is almost to the gun. Then start your swing, adjust the lead to no more than a foot and shoot it with a smooth swing about midway between the centre and the low house. Don't forget that this target, easy though it may appear, still needs a follow through.

Low house

English/NSSA
This is a bit trickier than the incomer. Point the gun where you expect the target to go, with the muzzles on its flight line. Although you can move as you call, it's best to see exactly where the target is going first. Some traps are inconsistent and this is just the station where you could be caught out. As soon as you've seen the target, point the gun straight at it and fire without trying to take a rifle style aim. Even taking your time you will break this target when it is no more than about 15 yards out of the trap.

Double

ISU
This is not a difficult pair, but the low house target does get away occasionally. It is important to see the target before you move, and not to react to the sound of the trap. See it, point the gun straight at it and fire the instant the gun beds into the shoulder.

Having shot the first target, the second will be well to the left of the muzzles. Reverse your swing, adjust the lead on the incomer to about a foot and with a smooth swing fire and follow through. Shoot this double with the same rhythm as all the others and you won't go far wrong.

English/NSSA
Having shot the singles, the double is just a repeat. Shoot the outgoer, pick up the incomer and, when the lead is adjusted and you are swinging smoothly, fire.

At English Skeet, assuming you haven't missed any to this point, you now have the option of shooting the high or the low target to make your 25. Most people choose the incomer since it is the easier. Give it full concentration, though, and make sure you break it.

Shooting the low house target on station 7

Station eight

ISU

These two targets allow very little time for the shooter to react, and because of this they can seem almost impossible to the newcomer. Exactly the same method will work on these targets as on any other, and they are actually a good deal easier than they first appear.

The feeling that they are very difficult comes from initially having a spectator's eye view of them. Seen from the sidelines, the target 'zooms' across the sky and is neatly shot well before it reaches the centre. It looks very difficult, but not from the shooter's viewpoint.

What he sees is a shallow quartering target, admittedly moving quickly, that needs a smooth but unhurried swing. Shooting it sustained lead makes it much easier than trying to shoot swing-through. Indeed, using the latter method I always feel there is an element of luck about it. Shooting sustained lead makes station eight relatively easy.

High house

Many stances have been adopted for this target. All the good ones have a single aim – to make the swing easy and free. A good stance is one that faces the centre peg. Point the gun here and then turn the body until the gun is pointing about six to eight feet out of the house, with the muzzles level with the shute.

Hold a soft focus just to the right of the house. Never look into the shute or you will not see the target until it's racing past your shoulder. Prepare yourself for instant reaction, then call for the target.

Don't think of moving until it appears, then get the muzzles moving ahead of it. Start mounting the gun at the same instant with the intention of having it fully mounted while the target is still coming to the centre peg. Many shooters take this target without rushing, half-way between the house and the centre peg.

You can shoot it with no more than about six inches of lead, but give it a foot for safety. As soon as the gun beds into position fire and follow through. There may seem to be no time to make these adjustments but there is, and much more than you would think. A good deal of practice is required to get to the stage where the target is under complete control.

NSSA

This target seems just as difficult to beginners as the ISU version, but it is seldom missed by experienced NSSA Skeet shooters. With the slower target the muzzles may be brought a fraction closer to the house prior to calling, which will give you that bit of extra time to shoot it. Look just outside the shute, eyes in soft focus, call for the target and lead it as it appears. Swing smoothly and easily, see the right lead and shoot immediately. The follow through is almost automatic.

Low house

ISU

This is the last target of the 25, and is possibly slightly more difficult than the high house target because it often comes out of an awkward background. Stand facing midway between the low house and the centre peg, then turn back to the house. Point the muzzles about six feet out from, and level with, the shute.

Avoid focusing on the background; hold a soft focus just to the left of the house and be fully prepared before calling for the target. As soon as it appears, start mounting the gun and begin moving the muzzles ahead of the target. As with the high target, the object is to get the gun fully mounted while the target is coming in, because once it gets beyond two-thirds of the way to the centre peg it starts getting tricky. Shoot the moment the gun comes firmly into the shoulder. The lead on this one is the same as for the high target. This low house target climbs quite steeply whereas the high house target flies relatively flat. It makes a difference to the feel of the two shots, and is something you will learn from practice.

NSSA

The same rules apply to this as to the ISU target. Background plays less of a part here because as soon as you call the target is on its way. Adjust the lead as you swing smoothly and fire as soon as the lead is right. If you have not missed any targets up until this stage you now get to shoot this one again for your 25 straight.

Station eight targets benefit from plenty of practice, so if you have access to a Skeet range and can get exclusive use of it, then take advantage of it. Practise carefully, take your time and try to remember what you are attempting to achieve. You will soon find that they are much friendlier than you imagined.

Training

Training of one sort or another is essential in any sport if a decent level of performance is first to be achieved and then maintained. Shooting is no exception. To be effective the training has to be suited to the game. Doing endless lengths of a swimming pool won't help a sprinter, for instance, and heaving slow, heavy weights is unlikely to help the shooter.

Let's look closer at the requirements. In shooting there is no explosive effort, no sudden violent movement. It needs neither great strength nor great speed. What the shooter must have is the ability to maintain concentration over a whole day, sometimes several days, and a degree of endurance, too. A clay shooter, to be any good, must also possess keen eyesight, excellent timing, good hand and eye co-ordination and conditioned reflexes.

Eyesight

Eyesight is determined genetically, and although it is a distinct advantage to have naturally good vision there are many very fine shooters who wear glasses or contact lenses. More important than the ability to see is the ability to change focus very quickly. This is particularly true where doubles are encountered, where the two targets can be at different ranges and travelling in opposite directions. An excellent eye exercise is to spend five minutes a day alternatively focusing on close objects and on those at greater distance. This is important for older shooters, who will find that without this sort of practice their eyes will take progressively longer to change focus, to the detriment of their shooting. There is a considerable difference between just seeing a target in the sky and actually holding it in sharp focus.

Co-ordination

Good co-ordination is again something you either have or you don't, and although there are some proficient shooters who are not good at other sports, most of the top shooters are sufficiently well co-ordinated to have performed well at other sports, too, particularly ball games. Playing sports like squash, badminton and tennis can do a lot for only average co-ordination.

Conditioned reflexes

Properly conditioned reflexes are the result of the correct application of good technique, coupled with plenty of practice. Good shooting relies on sound technique, but it is impossible to shoot well while trying to think about all the many things that constitute good technique. The ability to carry out a job of work well is directly related to how much of the work may be consigned to the subconscious. As an example of this, a good driver concentrates on the road ahead of him and behind him and relies on his conditioned reflexes to change gear, work the foot pedals, steer the car and to react in an emergency. Very often the driver's conditioned reflexes have him braking hard in a sudden emergency long before his conscious mind tells him to put his foot on the brake pedal.

Plenty of correct practice eventually drives good shooting technique into the subconscious, too. Much of the technique necessary to good shooting then becomes automatic, and the shooter can concentrate most of his attention on the target.

With an improvement in technique comes an apparent improvement in the speed of reaction. Actual reaction time to any situation is controlled by the amount of time it takes the brain to decide on a course of action. In a situation made familiar by constant repetition, the brain chooses this course much more quickly because the appropriate reaction is already well known. In this way good, regular shooting practice will see the shooter reacting far quicker than an untrained person could manage.

Of course, one point to remember is that the brain is just as ready to absorb bad technique as it is to learn good, and once learned it is difficult to unlearn. For this reason all beginners will benefit from a series of shooting lessons from a good coach. He will teach all the elementary but important aspects, such as gun mounting, and will watch carefully to make sure that the beginner develops his technique properly.

Once the basics are absorbed the shooter will have a good idea of what he is doing, and will have developed a feel of what he is doing, too. This is very important, because only by learning how each movement feels is the shooter able to reproduce it without thought.

Videos are a possibility as a training aid, and some coaches make use of the instant playback facility of modern video 'camcorders' to demonstrate to a shooter exactly what he is doing. Many shooters express shock when they first see themselves in this way. A smooth swing can look less so when exposed to the critical eye of the camera. Once the shooter has a firm impression of exactly what he is trying to achieve, then he can begin training properly.

Training

Going out with a big bag of cartridges and firing away at a couple of hundred targets is not training, although it might seem like it. 50 targets shot carefully will be far more beneficial. The intention of shooting training is to refine technique, improve scores and build confidence.

Confidence simply means having a generous portion of belief in one's own capabilities, and it doesn't necessarily apply only to winning. A confident shooter will also be realistic (though not resigned to failure!) about his abilities, and will recognise that during his early shooting days it is unrealistic to expect to win a competition outright. He will, however, be confident that his training methods are right, that he is gradually improving and that he will, sooner or later, be on that winner's rostrum.

Goal setting to improve scores

Setting yourself realistic goals, both in practice and in competition, is an excellent way towards rapid improvement and for gaining confidence. The key word here is 'realistic'. If, for instance, you are an Olympic Trap shooter with an average over your last 500 practice targets of 70%, then a realistic goal for your next 500 might be 75%. To set yourself a goal of 90% would not only be unrealistic but would almost certainly be unachievable. A 5% improvement is quite enough to aim for and only when that goal is attained can it then be raised again, perhaps to 79%. The goal in competition is then to shoot this average.

Gaining confidence

Developing confidence, that unshakeable self-belief, is all important. You must do everything you can to cultivate this powerful aid to good shooting and shun everything that can undo it. Confidence has nothing to do with brashness, and often the most brash elements in the shooting world are those who are least confident in their abilities. They confuse self-belief with self-delusion. Confidence can be improved in the following ways.

By setting realistic goals and attaining them.

By practising sound technique.

By always practising seriously, and only with others of like mind.

By not idolising top shooters to the point that you come to believe they are unbeatable.

By keeping accurate records of your performances so that you can study any weaknesses and work them out yourself or with a trusted instructor.

By ignoring what others say about certain targets or layouts. If you hear someone complaining, then you will know they've performed badly, and this means one less person that you will have to beat.

142

By accepting badly set targets as a challenge rather than as a focus for your complaints.

By being true to yourself through always doing your best and never giving up. However poorly you might have performed there is always some goal you can set yourself, even if it means avoiding coming last!

Positive thinking

Here are two series of advice for good shooting, both seemingly identical in their content but presented in two different ways.

Series one
1. I am not going to stand badly
2. I am not going to start with my gun in a poor position
3. I am not going to snap the gun to my shoulder
4. I am not going to dip the muzzles as I mount my gun
5. I am not going to take my eyes off the target
6. I am not going to swing jerkily
7. I am not going to stop my swing.

Series two
1. I am going to position myself carefully on each stand
2. I am going to ensure that the gun is in a good ready position
3. I am going to bring my gun smoothly to my shoulder
4. I am going to keep the muzzles on the line of the target during gun mounting
5. I am going to focus on the target throughout the shot
6. I am going to swing fluidly
7. I am going to follow through.

Looking at these two lists it appears that both say the same things, but they do not! As an example, look at number three in series one: 'I am not going to snap the gun to my shoulder'. What does this convey? That you intend throwing it on the ground? Or putting it back in the boot of your car? It is a negative statement that outlines only what must *not* be done, but not what *must* be done.

Look at number three in series two: 'I am going to bring the gun smoothly to my shoulder'. This gives the shooter a clear and positive message. Think positively.

Physical training methods

Playing games such as squash and tennis has already been mentioned as a fine training aid. General good health and a feeling of well-being are very important to any sport and anyone aspiring to the shooting heights must

Leading Sporting shot Denise Eyre improved her scores with regular workouts

be in good physical shape. Admittedly not all, but most leading shooters in the world are slim and reasonably fit and lead a relatively healthy life. If you are unfit, live on junk food, drink ten pints of lager a night and smoke heavily then you are certainly not doing yourself or your shooting any favours.

A programme of regular exercise can be fitted into the busiest day, and fifteen minutes set aside each morning or evening can soon become a very therapeutic antidote to the rigours and tensions of work. It will also help your shooting.

Whether or not you use weights in your training depends on your body type and your levels of natural strength. Many top shooters are naturally strong, even powerful men, who have more than enough strength and endurance to carry the modern clay gun throughout a long day's shooting. But there are just as many who would benefit from a regular work-out on a multi-gym, such as the type found at most leisure centres or health clubs.

A good all-round work-out is the thing to go for. The idea is to increase overall strength a few per cent and then maintain that improvement. Both women and men will benefit from a regular work-out with weights.

Training with the gun

If you only handle your gun when you are actually firing it, you will make slow progress. How many times do you fire your gun in practice? Perhaps 50 times, maybe 100? If so then you are taking a long time to do what could be achieved in fifteen minutes of practice without moving outside of your house, and which costs nothing, either. So-called 'dry practice' is one of the best ways of learning and maintaining good shooting technique. All you need is enough room to swing your gun and some snap caps.

The set-up

Before actually beginning any training with the gun make sure everything is right, from the feet up. Don't just grab your gun and start flinging it about. It's a waste of time and might do more harm than good. If you normally shoot in a jacket then put it on. If you shoot in trainers then wear them. Wear a hat if your normally shoot in one. The idea is to make everything feel exactly as it does when you are shooting.

Stand exactly as you would when shooting. Keep your feet relatively close together. They should never be more than a foot apart at the heels, and many tops shooters stand with their feet much closer together than this. Stand relaxed and upright, and make sure you are holding the gun properly.

Now adopt your ready position (depending on discipline), select a mark as an aiming point, and make a complete gun mount, pointing the gun at the mark. Then, repeat the exercise. The object is to do this as smoothly and correctly as possible. It is not an exercise in speed.

The purpose of doing this is to train the muscles that are used whenever a gun is mounted. It doesn't matter how often you lift weights, or how strong you eventually become; only regular exercise with your gun will train the right shooting muscles in precisely the right way.

Early on in your shooting career it will prove quite difficult to mount the gun properly, slowly, more than 20 or so times. By gradually increasing the number of times you can mount the gun before you tire, you will increase your skill in gun mounting, and you will gradually absorb how it feels when it's right.

The next stage is best carried out in a darkened room to avoid becoming pre-occupied with the barrels. The idea is to mount the gun as you are turning.

Basically your upper body will be making a standard gun mount. The only difference is that now your lower body will be turning to left or right as the gun is being mounted. This apparently simple movement is the very basis of good shooting.

So, standing in your good stance, practise this turn and mount. Always come right back to the ready position before starting a subsequent movement. Don't get into a kind of see-saw rhythmn. When you can do 25 full turns to the left and 25 to the right without tiring, then you are beginning to get somewhere.

Visualisation practice

Developing a strong mind is just as important as having a strong, healthy body. The ability to concentrate is vital, because a momentary loss of attention can cause the loss of a single target or a complete pair. The visualisation technique has been making great in-roads in remedial medicine, where as a form of self-hypnosis it has helped many people overcome or control serious medical problems. It also works well in sport, too.

The technique is well known in other sports, but is not widely used by clay shooters. It is exactly as it sounds: the imagination is used. It's a method of rehearsing your technique in your mind. There are many ways it can be employed. For instance the shooter can visualise himself to be a third person watching himself in action. Equally he can imagine himself actually shooting.

Before attempting this advanced method of training, the shooter will have developed a keen idea of what he is doing, and will have not just a feel for the technique but will have a good sight picture, an impression of how it all looks when everything is done properly and the shot succeeds. With these thoughts and pictures in mind the shooter can practice while sitting quietly in an armchair. He might, for instance, start with a simple target flying away. In his mind he walks on to the stand, loads the gun, gets into the ready position and calls for the target. As it flies away he smoothly mounts the gun, fires and watches it break. He then breaks the gun, ejects the cartridge, then goes through the routine again.

146

Kevin Gill demonstrates total concentration

Initially it is difficult to concentrate, and the mind will wander. Many people find it impossible to get past the first few imaginary shots, and without being aware that they have done it they will suddenly find that they are thinking about something else entirely, or even that they have fallen asleep. The trick is to pull your mind back and make it concentrate on the job at hand. Don't allow your mind to hop all over the place: decide

147

on a specific target or targets and stick with them until you are ready to change. If you cannot concentrate in the comfort of an armchair, with no distractions, how can you expect to do so at a proper shoot?

It is quite possible to do this exercise with the gun, preferably in a darkened room. Once again the targets are imaginary but everything else is real. Use the snap caps and fire the gun to help the timing of your imaginary shot. Most important, see the targets and see them break.

There are a lot of extensions of this technique. A good one is to imagine yourself needing just the last five targets to win a major competition. This can have an amazing effect after a while. Eventually you will find, if you are doing it properly, that your heart starts to race and the adrenalin begins to pump.

Shooting practice

There are two schools of thought on this subject. One says that the shooter should practise to attain a certain goal during a session, and having attained it he should stop. The other says that once attained the shooter should continue until the lesson is well and truly absorbed.

Which of these approaches you opt for depends on your own preference. Some shooters gain considerable reassurance from constantly repeating a successful shot or series of shots. Others will shoot perhaps two rounds in a day and settle for two 24s. I believe that the pressure of competition will lift your game enough to pick up that odd target. Some of my very best international scores have come after fairly indifferent practice sessions, with 24s interspersed with 23s and even 22s. Find which way suits you best and don't be influenced by other competitors one way or the other.

Advanced shooting training

There are many other methods whereby a shooter can improve his technique, some involving dry practice and others involving actual shooting. A very effective method, advocated by a number of leading shooting countries in Eastern Europe, is the shared target system.

In order for this to work effectively you need at least two, but better still, three shooters. As an example of how it works imagine a three man squad shooting ABT, with the shooters standing on pegs one, three and five.

Number one shooter loads his gun, mounts it and calls for the target. When it appears he shoots it as usual. Those shooters standing on pegs three and five also load their guns, but with snap caps. As the target appears, all shoot it in the normal way, but silently. Then the shooter on peg three shoots a target while the other two track it and fire using snap caps. The shooter on station five then has his go and when all three shooters have fired a shot they move up a peg and the practice is repeated until each has shot his 25 targets. At the end of the round each shooter will have shot at 25 targets but will have swung and silently fired his gun at another 50. For Skeet, stations one, two and three should be occupied to begin with, but the same rules apply, with each shooter taking his turn to shoot the targets on each station.

This has a very beneficial effect on the person actually shooting. Since he knows there are others tracking his target he tends to concentrate better and eventually learns to shoot sharply and smoothly. It also greatly helps the non-shooters, since they are able to take a proper shot in every respect except that they are not distracted by the gun firing. In this way good trigger pulling technique is learned, an important factor that is usually camouflaged by the recoiling of the gun. Many shooters using this method for the first time, are amazed how jerkily they pull the trigger when only using snap caps. In the right company, and only advanced shooters should practise this method, the target still breaks even though you haven't actually fired!

Sporting shooters can easily do this practice, although in all disciplines it is essential that the method is fully understood by those taking part. By far the best way is to do it under the supervision of a coach who is not shooting, otherwise it can become difficult to know who is doing what. Safety is, of course, paramount. Under no circumstances must live cartridges be used by anyone other than the one person actually shooting. It must never be used as a method to see who can break the target the quickest, since this is not only extremely dangerous but quite useless practice.

The methods outlined here are only a few of the many training techniques available that don't necessarily require the firing of lots of cartridges. They are not intended as a substitute for actual shooting but as a means of rapid improvement to be used in conjunction with proper shooting practice.

World women's no. 1 ISU Skeet shot, Svetlana Demina of the USSR

Ladies

As a generalisation, women fail to compete on equal terms with men in many sports, because they lack basic power or weight. In shooting there is no obvious reason why women don't compete at the same level, but with few exceptions the best women rarely achieve similar scores to the best men. It is difficult to understand why, unless you put it down to experience.

Many women are introduced to shooting by a boyfriend or husband. This means that they are likely to be in their late teens or twenties, young enough to enjoy shooting at a good level, but probably too old to learn to perform really well.

Most top male shooters have had access to guns since they were small children. I had an air rifle when I was six, had the use of a .22 rifle by the time I was ten, and was shooting a shotgun and fullbore rifles long before I left school. With that sort of background, clay shooting was a natural and easy progression. But even allowing that an early start is vital there is no reason why women shouldn't shoot a lot better than most of them do. Here are some ideas that might help.

Training

All the suggestions listed under the chapter on Training apply as much to women as to men, with the emphasis perhaps placed in different areas. One of the most important is strength. Mounting a gun once is easy for almost anyone, yet constant repetition, where the gun is mounted twenty times or more in quick succession, soon exposes muscles that need improvement. Shooting well is all about gun control, and if you cannot make the gun do exactly what you want, when you want, then you will not shoot to your maximum potential.

A regular twice weekly workout in a gymnasium is essential. Any descent establishment will offer advice on which machines to use, and how, and will give you a training schedule to follow according to your current skill and strength level. This will exercise and strengthen all parts of the body, and will greatly increase strength, speed and all round muscle firmness.

Along with power training, some form of reaction game should be played. Badminton and squash both require speed and dexterity and can also be played when outdoor tennis is impossible. This will improve eye and hand co-ordination and will also build stamina.

Shooting training

You cannot beat plenty of dry practice, and if you are determined enough you can increase your skill with the gun very quickly without firing a shot. Good gun handling is only a part of good shooting, but it is a very important part. Combined with sensible shooting training you will advance much quicker and surer than someone who only touches the gun when they take it out of its case to shoot it.

Once the basics of shooting have been absorbed one of the best disciplines to concentrate on is English Skeet. This teaches all the angles, the elements of good timing, the shooting of doubles, it makes you swing the gun properly, and it has the big advantage of being easy enough to ensure a fair score even in the early days. Once good scores at English Skeet are a regular occurrence then you are ready for anything, since you have learned how to control the gun.

Guns

Lightweight guns are easier to control but are more likely to cause discomfort from recoil. As long as sensible weight training is undertaken a normal weight gun will easily be handled, so it is best to go for those weighing about 7½ lb.

Guns are always made for right handed men, so unless you are particularly tall, you will need the stock shortened and the toe rounded off, not left pointed. At the same time it is a good idea to have one of the new recoil absorbing rubber pads fitted. They locate the gun nicely in your shoulder and stop it sliding about.

Women with small hands can be at a disadvantage with many guns. If it is impossible to wrap your hand around the pistol grip so that your thumb can easily rest on your middle finger, then you cannot control the rear end of the gun properly. A decent gunsmith can sort this out by reducing the thickness of the grip, and it is worthwhile having it done. Once you can unite finger and thumb with ease then it will remove all tension from the hand and make good 'triggering' much easier.

Most women shoot 12 bore guns

The fore-end of the gun can also be beneficially slimmed down, again so that control is easier. Recoil is not absorbed wholly by the shoulder. In fact most of it, once you have learned how to shoot properly, is taken through the hands and arms. This is a purely instinctive thing that will be impossible if the hands cannot grip properly.

Twenty bore guns

Now that shot loads have been reduced to one ounce for nearly all disciplines, the prospect of using a 20 bore looms large for some women. They are lighter, take a lighter cartridge and have correspondingly less recoil. Unfortunately they are also a handicap in that they put less lead in the air.

This drawback will be completely balanced out if you simply cannot handle a 12 bore, and at a discipline like Skeet it is likely that the smaller calibre is no handicap at all. Of course you can get one ounce load 20s if you want to shoot Sporting or Trap, but if you want to shoot these heavy weight 20s then you are back with recoil problems and you would do better with a 12 bore.

Goals

If women have enough ambition and sufficient talent, there is no reason why they should not compete equally with men. Olympic Trap shooter Susan Nattrass of Canada has several times finished in the top ten overall in major championships, including the world event, while Soviet ISU Skeet lady Svetlana Demina regularly shoots scores most men can only dream about. Only the vagaries of the rule book prevented her from winning a major championship outright in the late 1980s, when she had shot 198×200! In Sporting there are a number of women who equal men's scores.

If you take your shooting seriously then get training, do plenty of home practice with the gun and watch those scores improve. You are limited only by your personal level of determination.

Competition

You can practise repeatedly, and acquire a good style but the real test lies in competition. Unless you compete seriously you will never really know how good you are. There are very many club shooters who appear to be world beaters. They seldom miss a target during a club shoot, and the general opinion is that if they ever went out and joined the competition circuit they would take it by storm. Perhaps they would, but more likely they wouldn't, at least not straight away.

There is a big difference between shooting for fun and shooting in competition. In the former it doesn't really matter whether or not you shoot well, and so the pressure of having to perform to a good standard is removed. The likelihood is that with reasonable talent you will shoot well. In a competition there are many additional pressures which can help rather than hinder your performance, providing you learn to channel

East German Axel Wegner being congratulated after winning an ISU Skeet Olympic Gold medal

them properly. Under the pressure of competition, assuming you have your thoughts and feelings under control, adrenalin floods the system, eyesight sharpens and so do reflexes. For some people, however, the pressure becomes too much and instead of their performances improving they find they can hardly load the gun! What are the pressures, what causes them, and how can they be brought under control?

Some are created by the presence of onlookers and other shooters. No-one wants to look a fool in front of friends or strangers. Some are created by the desire to produce a good score. If a shooter is running up a particularly good score, one that might actually win, then that creates additional pressure. These pressures exist only in the mind of the shooter, and are all caused by a fear of failure. Be positive and regard competition as a chance to show your true worth.

Don't worry about what others think. Most shooters only watch the targets of the preceding shooter so that they can form an idea of what they themselves are going to do. Whether or not you hit the targets is usually of no interest to anyone other than the referee, and yourself. With one stand or one round to go, if you are leading an event, the majority of spectators will want you to do well. The only ill wishers might be the few who could beat you, but that's only to be expected. Ignore casual spectators who probably don't know good shooting from bad.

Always remember to shoot one target at a time. Forget what has gone before and don't worry about the next shot. Don't allow the fact that you missed the previous target make you miss others.

The same advice holds true when you find yourself in a potential winning position. You can only break one target at a time. Don't think about all the remaining targets or you will start missing shots.

The wonderful thing about clay shooting is that you can wrap yourself in complete concentration and shoot great scores if you have the ability, without being aware of what others are doing. You get the opportunity to run up a score on exactly the same targets as everyone else, without any hindrance other than that imposed by the targets themselves, or by your own inhibitions.

Getting ready

Plenty of shooters arrive at the last minute for their squad, forgetting their ear muffs or shooting glasses, perhaps even their gun. It is no surprise when they proceed to shoot badly.

With the exception of English Sporting, all disciplines require the shooter to be ready for his squad at a certain time. It makes sense to keep an eye on the squad board and to start getting ready at least fifteen minutes before you are due to shoot. Then you can be sure that you have everything you need, and can arrive at your own pace and look at the targets of the squad shooting before you.

A few years ago at a European Championship a very famous French shooter mis-read the squad board and arrived in time to see his squad shooting their final few targets. By ISU rules this meant that he automatically lost three targets. These were to prove very important. Had he not lost them he would have won the European Championship outright and France would have won the team gold. As it was he finished fifth and France finished out of the medals. This was a hard lesson he was not allowed to forget in a hurry.

Pre-shoot training

At major competitions there is always a period prior to the event when shooters are allowed to train. At Grands Prix this may be as little as one day. At events of European Championship status and above three days is more usual. It is important to use this period wisely.

At Sporting there is little chance that you will train on the actual stands used in the event. The training period is really for loosening up, getting travel weariness out of yourself and getting the feel of the place.

Skeet and Trap shooters always train on the stands and targets that will be used in the event, and it is important that they do. Although the targets will fly little differently to those shot at home there are many variations that can cause problems. These are as follows:

Target colour

Target colour can be anything the organisers care to make it. If you have trained on orange and find the competition is to be held using yellow then you will need to get used to this difference.

Target speed

Target speed can vary with atmospheric pressure. A shooting ground at high altitude will throw very different targets to one at sea level, even though both conform to the rules.

Target visibility

Target visibility is a combination of colour and background. Many home shooting grounds have very open backgrounds, whereas abroad the background can be anything from wide open to rocks or dark forest. Any variation takes a little getting used to.

Temperature

Temperature can be very high in some countries, and extremely draining. The trick is to drink lots of liquids, including the electrolyte drinks, and to wear a hat of some sort.

Types of trap used

For Skeet shooters the type of traps used can sometimes cause problems. Most Skeet shooters get used to reacting not only to the target but also to the sound of the trap. A totally silent trap takes some getting used to!

How much a shooter should train during the period allotted is a matter of personal requirement, but it is surely better to do too little than too much. Remember that these are training and not practice periods, and if you cannot hit some targets at this stage then it is a bit late to start worrying about it. To shoot 150 to 200 targets each day, as some do, is patently absurd. If you have no problems why go looking for them? I remember someone shooting endless streams of 25s in the training period at one World Championship, and yet he only managed to shoot a 187×200 in the actual event. He had effectively shot himself out.

The shoot-off

Many shooters greatly fear shoot-offs, and as a result they lose before they fire the first shot. In this situation, ask yourself if you really believe that you deserve to win. Do you really want to win? Can you accept the responsibility of winning? An American Football coach once said: 'Winning is not the most important thing: it's the *only* thing.' This is the professional view of a highly paid sport, and perhaps such an uncompromising approach should not be applied to an amateur sport like clay shooting. However, there is an underlying truth there that possibly applies to all sports.

Winning is more a state of mind than it is a reflection of ability. There are many shooters with great ability who never win, while there are others with less ability who win all the time. It's all a question of attitude of mind, and someone with a winner's mentality will be positive in his approach, combative in his outlook (to competition) and will never give up.

If you don't think you deserve to win, and cannot accept the responsibility of being champion, what are you doing out there? You already have proven ability to be in the shoot-off. But don't let the other shooter's ability and his reputation put you off. Think positively, believe you can win and concentrate on each target in turn. Think your way into winning!

Index